MAN AND
HIS KIND

MAN AND HIS KIND

Thomas Crump

PRAEGER PUBLISHERS
New York · Washington

ACKNOWLEDGEMENT

The Publishers acknowledge the permission of the Clarendon Press to reproduce the illustration on p. 124 which originally appeared in *Divinity and Experience* by R. G. Lienhardt.

BOOKS THAT MATTER

Published in the United States of America in 1973
by Praeger Publishers, Inc.
111 Fourth Avenue, New York, N.Y. 10003

© 1973 in London, England, by Thomas Crump

Library of Congress Catalog Card Number: 73–7836

Printed in the United States of America

CONTENTS

1

The Individual and Society: the World and Cosmos

Social anthropology is the study of man in society. Its interest in the individual is primarily in the roles which society may allocate to him. Individual psychology is largely outside its scope, but society itself is an abstract concept, and it could not exist apart from the individuals who are its members. We must therefore guard against the 'fallacy of misplaced concreteness'—heeding the warning of the philosopher A. N. Whitehead. At the same time science only advances by making useful abstractions from the facts before it— and the institutions of society which interest the anthropologist are of this kind. But since these institutions, whatever they are, or whatever their purpose, only operate by virtue of the interaction of different individuals, we are ourselves involved in them to a degree which, judged scientifically, is very exaggerated.

Any approach which we make to our subject is bound to be conditioned by our whole cultural inheritance. If we study, say, pure mathematics, it may matter little whether we are English or French, or of any other nationality—or culture, to use the word which anthropologists prefer. In anthropology it matters profoundly. For we must first appreciate the character of the anthropological folk-lore which we have acquired, and continue to acquire, almost unconsciously, throughout our lives.[1] This includes all those prejudicial ideas which we have as much about ourselves as about others. Thus we may see ourselves with our own particular virtues, where we deny them (which may be seen as such only because of our cultural inheritance) even to some of our closest neighbours.

To start with, we must have some idea of what we mean by 'society'. It may be seen as any group of people living in common, sharing with each other certain fundamental attitudes, beliefs and practices. The idea presupposes a definite unity about things of basic importance in day-to-day life.

It is impossible to generalize about the number of members there must be to make up a society. In a sense the whole of China, with 750,000,000 people, is one society: in another sense a married couple and their children might be said to form a society. What really defines a society is a high degree of cohesion within itself, together with differentiation from any persons or groups outside it. A family, in practice, is never a meaningful society in this sense, because it will share its 'culture'—a term to be defined later—with numerous other families. To find out what society we are members of we must ask ourselves this sort of question: What is the group of people whose way of life, in comparison with that of all other people, is basically the same as our own?

Now in the complex world of advanced technology, which is really the only world which most of us know, this question may be answered at a number of different levels. For some purposes it is decisive that one comes from a particular home-town, for others that one is a member of a certain profession—perhaps with international connections—for others that one is a graduate of a certain university, and so on. For reasons of this kind anthropologists prefer to study simple groups, where the society of which they are part is uniquely and obviously defined. The ideal is a remote island, with a small homogeneous population, subject to no outside influences: such in fact is the Polynesian island of Tikopia, whose 1,000-odd inhabitants have been studied by Firth in astonishing detail.[2] Significantly, when we come to study such societies, we find that the institutions through which they are organized do not necessarily have anything in common with the institutions which we are familiar with in the Western world. Many anthropologists have ceased to take their bearings from any of the institutions of their own society. This has the virtue of scientific detachment, but at the cost, perhaps, of making the basic ethnographic material remote and somewhat esoteric.[3]

Man, a 'higher primate' in zoological terms, organizes his societies on an unprecedented scale. Some other primates do live in groups larger than that of the family, however extended—baboons, for instance, in troops up to 200.[4] This is the maximum extent of their society and it would be difficult to find a human society as small. The Tikopia have already been noted. The Todas of South India, studied by Rivers some sixty years ago, numbered less than a thousand.[5] Lévi-Straus found in Brazil a few even smaller societies, but they appear to be becoming extinct, and this is very significant.[6]

The fact is that man, as a species, cannot, apparently, live on too small a scale, socially speaking. No individual will know every member of his society—however small it is—but the individual members of any society will be dependent upon each other in a way essential to their survival. This is true, even though most of the year may be spent in very small groups, perhaps no greater than a single family.

Now it is next to impossible to say definitely why all this should be. We can, however, look briefly at man as an animal species, paying particular attention to the mentality and physiology of the individual. It should first be *underlined*—although we may regret the need to do so—that we are talking about a unique animal species, not as such capable of being sub-divided in any significant way. Anyone with prejudices at this level, about such matters as race, will not easily understand social anthropology.

Now man, as an individual, is so incapacitated by mental and physical immaturity during the first years of his life, that he can only survive with the help of continuous care and nourishment from adult members of his species.[7] At the same time his physique is so unspecialized that he can adapt himself to life in a range of *habitat* far wider than that of any other form of life.[7] Intellectually man has uniquely wide powers of communication, learning and memory —the three going naturally together. Now the factors mentioned in this paragraph may together require man always to live in relatively large scale societies, but if so, they give him also the means to organize his life in a manner infinitely more complex than that of any other species. For although each of these natural human attributes may be found in other species, there will always be such differences in degree as to make man a totally different kind. The real break is between the baboon and aboriginal man, and not between aboriginal man and man as a member of a complex advanced technological society. The social anthropology of baboons could only be a significant subject for study at a very low level of analysis. But the same subject for man—however primitive—is of endless complexity and fascination, and a book such as this one can do no more than sketch it in outline.

NATURE, CULTURE AND TECHNOLOGY

Three concepts will constantly recur in the course of this study. They are nature, culture and technology. Nature is concerned with those things which are true about the whole species of man, and substantially every member of it, of whatever tribe or nation, and whenever, in the history of the world, he may live. Now man by his nature has a body, and most particularly a brain, which function in certain immutable ways. These give very considerable powers to man in society, but the way in which these powers may develop and be applied in any one society is invariably highly specialized—much more so than the normal man appreciates.

In the somewhat narrow sense in which anthropology uses the word 'nature' it is impossible to make any such statement as 'Englishmen are *naturally* phlegmatic'. As a natural phenomenon *phlegm* (itself not a very scientific concept) could only be an attribute of all human kind. If it is exclusive to the English, and one or two other peoples, it can only be a *cultural* attribute, for the attributes of man which are the concern of culture are defined not for the whole species, but differently for every society. And culture is of far greater interest to anthropology than nature.

Every society has a culture, and it is inherently the creation of the society itself, rather than of any individual members of it. Culture comprehends every kind of human behaviour. It includes speech and language, table manners and the preparation of food, morality, religion and mythology. And this list is far from exhaustive. Almost any human, as opposed to animal, institution falls within the definition of culture. Even *natural* human actions, such as eating and copulation, are invariably transformed by cultural accretions.

To the anthropologist the fact that man eats is in itself almost trivial: we are not interested in human metabolism. It is the actual food that man eats, and how he prepares it, and all kinds of related questions, differing from one society to the next, which are really critical.[8] The same is true of man's sexual life.

Culture, then, even if concerned with man's coming to terms with his own nature or with the world around him, is much more an autonomous aspect of his essential social life. Man always has more culture than he needs: his cultural institutions can never be wholly explained simply by the need to come to terms with his natural environment. They are much more a product of the human environment. Indeed, language, the most abstract of all cultural institutions, has no natural basis beyond man's capacity to articulate sound. It is culture—as exemplified by the myth of the Tower of Babel[9]—which divides man into different kinds, each one of which is then preoccupied with maintaining its own cultural boundaries. At one level the different culture-groups of man may be compared to different animal species,[10] but with this difference, that any one such group is liable to be assimilated to any other, or to change its essential institutions in the face of any external process—natural or political. It is this which makes the idea of cultural evolution—greatly favoured by nineteenth-century anthropologists—so misleading. Culture goes so far beyond being a means of adaptation to natural environment, that the forces which change it are simply not of the same kind as those which shape the evolution of any natural species.

'Culture' itself is a concept of culture: it is scarcely 'natural' even to *homo sapiens*, although it is his unique attribute. Yet to any man, it is his 'cultural' rather than his 'natural' world which really matters.

It is fundamentally wrong to talk of culture in quantitative terms: we must not say that the Dinka[11] of the Southern Sudan have more culture (or indeed less) than the Tikopia,[12] nor that the religion of one is superior (or inferior) to that of the other. More generally it is misleading to categorize societies as 'advanced' or 'primitive'. True enough, this is commonly done, not only in English society, but in countless others—including particularly those which we are inclined to think of as *primitive*—but it is still hopelessly unscientific.

We can still make quantitative comparisons between different societies. For every society will have its own technology (indeed as a part of its culture) and this will be *advanced* or *primitive* to the degree that it enables the local environment to be subdued and made productive of all the material things, from roots dug out of the ground for food, to space-ships which land on the moon, such as man pleases to enjoy. The terms 'advanced' and 'primitive' are too useful to be neglected, so it is in this technological sense that they will be used in this book.

An increase of social organization always goes with technological advance. A primitive society may have a very large population, but it will then be capable of being sub-divided, down an ever decreasing scale, into smaller social systems, each with the same essential organization.[13] This is the 'mechanical' property of the primitive segmentary society.[14] The technologically advanced society is essentially 'organic';[15] no part of it can exist on its own. It does divide into separately functioning components. It has much more a highly articulated structure, in which every part is significant only for its interaction with all the others. This requires social organization on a massive scale: the United Kingdom, with more than fifty million inhabitants, is less an independent society than any of Lévi-Strauss's Brazilian tribes, with its mere handful of members.

THE MODEL OF A STABLE SOCIETY

Paradoxically, although history shows how open any culture is to change, we are forced to assume—at least of any pre-literate society —that it is stable and uniform. It is significant that the members of any such society will be very strongly inclined to make precisely these assumptions about it, even in the face of the clearest social or historical evidence to the contrary. Instability and diversity are almost terms of insult. They are certainly complicating factors to the social anthropologist, and they go a long way to explain his preference, already noted, for the study of simple, stable and isolated societies. These so-called 'global'[16] societies provide the best laboratory for the fundamental research which the subject depends upon.

There are a number of processes specifically directed to maintaining the stability of a primitive society. These are known as 'homeostatic', and their concern is with the integrity of the local culture. They will not all have the same force in every primitive society, but they will still be far more critical than they could ever be in an advanced complex society. Of these processes some will focus on the ecology,[17] that is, the physical and biological environment of the society, and others on the social and cultural organization.

On the ecological side, the country itself may be extremely poor in natural resources. The Dinka[18] live in a land without any iron or stone. Their material possessions, such as their houses and cattle byres, are made from mud, grass and wood, and are extremely perishable. They wear little clothing. Their most durable possessions are probably metal spears, which play an important part in their culture. The climate only allows for a very limited range of food production, based on simple cultivation of millet, seasonal fishing, and the herding of cattle on a considerable scale—but in practice for reasons which are mainly religious and social.

Among the Dinka almost all the men look after the cattle, and find the raw materials for food, while the women prepare the food and look after the children. One or two specialized religious and political roles are confined to a minority only of the population, but the main role-differentiation is between the two sexes—an almost invariable feature of such societies, in contrast to our own, with its countless different occupations.[19]

To develop further the present contrast, the behaviour of members of any primitive society is predictable to a degree much greater than with an advanced society, while, at the same time, they are constantly at the mercy of unpredictable natural forces, such as flood, storm, drought, famine and disease.

Primitive society must therefore maintain the stability of its institutions in the face of the material instability of daily life. It is difficult for us to conceive of a people such as the Dinka, who possess hardly any kind of durable material property. Such a society is then much concerned to create durable cultural property, preserved by the constant re-enactment of the right ritual. (Consider—in Catholicism—how the ritual of the Mass preserves the integrity of sacramental theology.) The Dinka—and other like societies—have then little room for the individualist, the man who wishes to take an initiative and do something on his own, or in a different way to that hallowed by tradition.

The individual personality tends to be effaced, and much more the organization of society will depend on certain recognized groups; the smallest being the family. This has the advantage of creating more permanent units in the fabric of the society. A family may survive indefinitely, even though each individual member of it in time will die. In practice the family as such is not a very convenient group for a society whose structure is based on the relationship of different groups among themselves. There are other kinship-based groups which better serve this purpose, and they will be considered in Chapter 2.

The norms governing the relationships between different groups will themselves be a part of the cultural inheritance of the society. These relationships will seldom be modified by any *ad hoc* agreement made between two or more such groups, and the same will be true of the relationships between individuals, whether or not fellow members of any recognized group. Here the important concept is *status*, which in advanced societies gives way to that of *contract*.[20] For contract imports the possibility of changing social relationships deliberately, which is bound to be a socially disruptive event, even if on a very small scale. This possibility is too much for the fragile structures of primitive people. For such folk, subject always to natural forces which they can hardly master, predictable human behaviour, according to unquestioned rules and often enforced by religious sanctions, is absolutely essential. This is the subject of Chapters 6 and 8.

Stability, therefore, is more than an attribute of primitive society, convenient for the anthropologist. Homeostatic processes are the essence of primitive culture, which, without any form of written record, can only interpret the world existentially, and without any historical perspective. So the people of a primitive society are always concerned to act out the same play. The homeostatic processes ensure that the 'right lines' are taught to each new generation. There are indeed such processes in any society, but in one such as our own they must contend with others almost consciously directed towards re-writing the play for its next performance.

It is essentially a question of equilibrium. The extent of the contrast between the two poles may be illustrated by comparing the changes which our own society has undergone in the course of a single generation, with the social and cultural state of the Tiwi[21]—islanders off Northern Australia—which, according to the ethnography, was substantially *unchanged* for the whole of their first 14,000-odd years in their present habitat. Yet so frail were their institutions, that they have been largely effaced by barely half a century of Australian colonial administration. There must be a moral in this somewhere.

THE PRIMITIVE WORLD VIEW

So far our view of any society has been confined to its own members and within its own geographical frontiers. But what do primitive people think of the outside world? This will depend on the sort of contact which they have with other people than themselves. If they are like the Tikopia, before the arrival of the first Europeans, they will have no direct experience of any such people.[22] At the other extreme there are primitive societies which have very close contacts with other cultures. The Mbuti Pygmies of Zaire, for instance, spend part of the year in the forest, where no-one ever disturbs them, but the rest of the year in surrounding villages, where their lives are closely interwoven with those of the Bantu villagers. This case is particularly interesting for the way in which the local Bantu can conceive of the Pygmy social organization only in terms of their own, whereas the two are essentially different from each other.[23]

Most primitive peoples fall between the two extremes. Remote islands such as Tikopia are exceptional, however much they may delight the anthropologist. But even 'continental' tribes are likely to have very little contact with their neighbours, particularly in comparison with their internal commerce. By and large one tribe will not marry its women into another: indeed the whole culture of a neighbouring tribe, including its language, is likely to be largely unknown. This is not to say that the members of one tribe will not have a sort of folk-lore concerning their immediate neighbours. They almost certainly will. Indeed they may see their own tribal origins in the migration of a segment of the population of a neighbouring tribe.[24] Such myths of origin may even have a historical basis. The practice of adopting members of a neighbouring tribe as members of one's own tribe is reasonably common, and this may follow forcible abduction in the course of what is scarcely more than a slave-raid. War and cattle-raiding may also provide contacts with neighbouring peoples, and doubtless they add to the folk-lore concerning them, as any old soldier with foreign service will confirm.

In every direction the world-view of primitive peoples shades very rapidly into complete unreality, as Chapter 8 will make clear. The time frontier with the unknown is as close as the space frontier. Primitive history seldom has a span of more than three or four generations. Some peoples, such as the Tiv of Nigeria, must trace their ancestors further back than this, if they are to maintain their kinship systems.[25] This is relatively uncommon, except for the case of the founding ancestors of clans, and even more, of royal dynasties, where they exist. The basis of such genealogies is mythopoeic rather than historical. The five to six thousand years which Archbishop Ussher, in the seventeenth century, insisted was the time which had elapsed since the days of Adam and Eve, would be quite exceptional for a primitive society. But then His Grace made his calculations at the dawn of the age of enlightenment, and they were based entirely on written records.[26] The societies of interest to anthropology are almost entirely without the written word, and this makes a world of difference as Chapter 7 will illustrate.

This is not to say that primitive man is without communication. Language, the most complex and versatile means of communication, is a subject of endless fascination. Yet without writing, or more the permanent record which writing alone can provide, words are ephemeral, liable only to be carried away on the wind. The spatio-temporal frontiers of the pre-literate world are correspondingly circumscribed.

Yet primitive man transcends these limitations by a means which, if our own scientific world repudiates it, none the less gives a cosmic power to his ideals. This means is the language of myth, for the stories it tells, in endless variation, transmit themselves across the centuries, from a time far beyond the historical memory of any who hearken to them. The language of narration may change, there may be countless variations in presentation, but the essential content always stays the same. So also, primitive cultures use symbolism very creatively, and in a way which enormously enhances the meaning of their social and, more particularly, their religious institutions. This whole subject will be taken up again in Chapter 7, which is about communication: it relates also to Chapter 8, which is concerned with primitive religion.

So primitive man has also a cosmology—a view or an interpretation of the universe. But where we see the universe governed by science, or the natural law as we may choose to call it, primitive man sees the world governed by moral or ritual laws, which are considered in Chapters 5 and 8. This fact is implicit in almost all primitive culture, and without a proper understanding of it, the world of primitive man cannot be grasped. It explains why, in looking at any primitive institution—social, cultural, political, religious or economic —it can be misleading to take our bearings from a similar institution in our own society. The facts, abundantly gathered by workers in the field, must be allowed to speak for themselves. The anthropologist's job is to interpret them, if necessary by means of accepted models of social and cultural organization, but without imposing upon them his own preconceptions as to what story they should tell. It is a real problem for the anthropologist to know how to relate the essential orderliness of scientific method to the diverse and heterogeneous material which he chooses to study. Without resolving this problem, at least partially, anthropology will reduce at one extreme to being no more than a travelogue about remote peoples with strange and exotic customs, and the other to providing no more than abstract models of society, unrelated to any observed facts. In the rest of this book, the reader must almost consciously follow a middle way, if he is to understand what anthropology is about.

2

Marriage and the Family: Kinship and Affinity

THE FAMILY AND THE INDIVIDUAL

A mere handful of people, not all of the same generation, living together, and far more dependent on each other than they are on any outsider, will generally make up the smallest group in any society. This we will call the 'domestic group'. In all but exceptional cases most, if not all, of its members will live together in one 'homestead' and belong to one 'family'. 'Homestead' and 'family' are put in inverted commas because anthropology can hardly give them any precise meaning. They should certainly not be interpreted according to their meaning—which is itself uncertain enough—in our own society.

At this stage there is no need to define 'homestead' as anything but the place where the domestic group normally lives together. It may comprise one building, or even a part of building, or a compound containing a number of separate huts: indeed it may have no fixed structures of any kind. The family must be more precisely defined. To begin with there is the 'elementary' or 'nuclear' family, which is at the centre of the domestic group in almost every society. Taking the symbol △ to represent the male and ○ the female, the elementary family will consist of a 'married' couple and their 'infant' children, as shown in this diagram:

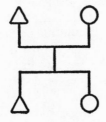

(The line joining the male and the female in the top row means that they are 'married' and are the 'parents' of the 'children' in the bottom row. The vertical line therefore represents *descent*, a very important anthropological concept, which will be discussed later. It is immaterial that the diagram shows one male and one female child: this is clearly only one possibility. For the present, also, 'marriage' and 'parenthood' must be left undefined.)

The children in the diagram are taken to be 'infants', in the sense that they are not yet old enough to have left home to start their own families.

Where, as is common enough in primitive societies, one man has several wives, he will be the father in a number of elementary families, which together will form a 'compound' family. Typically, in a case of this kind, each wife will have a hut of her own, to bring up her own family, in a common compound. Here the basic unit could be said to be the individual mother and her children, with the common father only loosely attached to it.

The compound family still consists of only two generations: the domestic group commonly goes further than this, so as to include members of three generations. This is the case of the 'extended' family, which may be all that the domestic group consists of. But such a group may also include a handful of members only distantly related, if indeed at all, to the family at the centre of it, so becoming a complete 'domestic group'.

In the conditions of primitive life, the domestic group is the fundamental social unit. It will include members of both sexes, in more or less equal numbers, and of varying ages. The part to be played by every member will be defined by the culture of the wider society, in which one domestic group will function very much like any other. Almost certainly the tasks allotted to the men will be different from those of the women: the roles of the two sexes will be complementary rather than co-operative. (It is surprising how little primitive men and women seem to see of each other.) And the younger children, once capable of assuming them, will have their own special duties. From the natural resources available to the group, which may all be culled from a limited geographical area assigned to it, at least the greater part of its material needs will be met. The picture is of complete domestic self-sufficiency. What, then, is there to spoil the idyll?

The answer is in the early chapters of the book of Genesis, and also in the mythology of countless primitive peoples. For God's judgment on Eve is that she shall 'bring forth children',[1] and to Adam (who represents all humanity) he declares, 'you are dust, and to dust you shall return'.[2] Our mortality is compensated by our powers of procreation. This means for the domestic group that the relationships within it are continually changing. From day to day the round of its activities may hardly seem to change. Yet it cannot ever escape from a succession of crises. New members are born into it: old members die. Others may leave to form new groups of their own, most commonly because their own families can no longer fit into their original home.

The stages in the life of any group may be described as expansion, fission and replacement:[3] expansion, because of the birth of new children; fission, because older children move away with families of their own; and replacement, because at the end of the day, perhaps with the death of the last survivor of an older generation, the group finally disintegrates, and other newer ones take its place.

The crises which occur within a domestic group relate to individual members of it.[4] The first life-crisis is birth. The mother of the new-born child may be kept in ritual seclusion, awaiting a purification ceremony to cleanse her from the inevitable impurity of her condition. At the same time the child must pass through a rite of initiation before it becomes a recognized member of the family and society into which it is born.

Adolescence is the occasion of another crisis, when another ceremony will commonly admit the child to a new rank in society so it will thereafter play an adult role, quite different from that assigned to it throughout its childhood. This may require the new initiate to live in a different place, in entirely new company, with special tasks assigned to it in the day to day life of the community.[5]

Marriage—to be looked at in the next section—and the birth of children to the marriage (already considered above) are the occasions of yet further crises, leading at one stage or another to a new domestic group being set up.

And death is the greatest crisis of all, for the group as much as for the individual. Funeral rites, or mortuary customs as they are more commonly known, are generally the most elaborate and long drawn out in any primitive community. For the deceased they declare ritually his departure from his earthly home, and assure his admission into another other-worldly resting place. For his family and community the rites ensure that life will go on, without the dead man returning—in ghostly form—to create any kind of unrest,

In the domestic groups, as so far considered, we see no enduring social institution. But some permanent institutions are essential even for the lowest possible level of social organization. In our own society we take such institutions for granted: the modern corporate state with its central government, supported by numerous official agencies, surrounded by countless limited companies, trusts, foundations and so on, provides a social matrix in which the family and the individual can each go their own way without any other basic structures to sustain them. This is the welfare state, but it is hardly the state of any primitive people. In primitive society permanent structures are developed by an extension of concepts of family and kinship. But first, before there can be any family or any kin, there must be the institution of marriage, and the procreation of children within it.

SEX AND MARRIAGE

Every society has its own understanding of sex and marriage, our own not less than any other. The whole subject is bedevilled by moral conditions, varying widely from one culture to another, but with each separate and distinct culture assuming a universal validity for its own code of conduct.

The understanding of our own society will be taken as the point of departure, however contrary this may be to the principle stated at the end of Chapter 1. This is only because there must be some reference point. It is not because our own standards can claim to regulate those of any primitive people. Now sex may be taken to be a biological phenomenon—whereby new life is created—and marriage, a social institution, to be found in every society.

Our knowledge of sex may be summed up in two principles:

1. A single act of coitus, at the right stage in the woman's fertility cycle, is all that is necessary for procreation.
2. The child born as a result of such an act will inherit physical characteristics from both parents.

Neither of these two principles is generally accepted in primitive society. For instance, Malinowski concluded from his study of the Trobriand islanders that they did not realize that the male role was essential to procreation:[6] other societies believe that successive acts of coitus, throughout the whole pregnancy, are necessary for the growth of the unborn child.[7] Very often, although the part played by the man is recognized as necessary, it is not seen as sufficient of itself: a spirit is also needed to enter the woman's body for conception to take place.[8] The possible types of primitive sexology are far too varied for them all to be considered.

Primitive understanding of heredity is equally diverse. Very often the child is seen as inheriting its physical characteristics only from one parent. If this is the man (known as the *genitor*, who will not necessarily be the *father*), the woman provides in her womb no more than the place in which the man's seed develops into the form of the child at birth. Where the woman (who may nearly always be taken as both *genitrix* and *mother*) alone bestows upon the child its biological inheritance, the man does no more than open up the womb so that it can generate the child and nourish it with his semen until it is ready to be born.

Let us now turn to marriage, a much more important matter for the social anthropologist, who after all is interested in society much more than in physiology. We think of marriage as a *permanent* relationship between a man and a woman, entered into by their own free choice (generally because they believe they are 'in love'), being of relatively little concern to anyone else (except possibly to any children who *may* be born), and providing the only legitimate context for a physical sexual relationship.[9] True, we recognize divorce and remarriage, but only as exceptional cases, and also the *marriage de convenance* and the shot-gun marriage, which are hardly categories in primitive thought. Our society rejects polygamy in every shape and form, and also the idea that women, as marriage partners, are at the disposal of the male members of the group into which they are born. Such things are quite normal in any number of primitive societies.

Now anthropologists have been at something of a loss to define marriage. The following definition is probably the best they have reached so far:

> Marriage is a union between a man and a woman such that children born to the woman are recognised legitimate offspring of both parents.[10]

This definition does not require that the parents live together. Often enough in primitive societies adult men live largely apart from the women. Nor is it necessary that the children should be begotten by their 'father', in the sense of the male parent recognized as such in the local society. Indeed, in one or two exceptional cases, of which the best known comes from the Nuer of the Southern

Sudan, the 'father' may in fact be another woman.[11] But most important of all, and implicit in the above definition, is the existence of children. This factor, more than any other, makes of marriage a uniquely significant social institution, and not just the socially approved context for sexual relations. Plainly in the Nuer case of woman-to-woman marriage, it is with someone other than the 'father' that the 'mother' has sexual relations if she conceives a child to be born of the marriage.

(The reader must not think that primitive societies enjoy unrestricted sexual licence. In fact sexual behaviour is subject to every kind of control and restriction. A man is generally entitled to the exclusive sexual services of his wives, and any trespasser against this title will be an adulterer. Even coitus with a wife will sometimes be forbidden, in a prescribed period before or after child-birth, for example.)

There is one classic case of 'marriage' which, although it requires the definition given above to be somewhat extended, at the same time illustrates its application. The Nayars form a caste on the Malabar coast of South India.[12] Now in the eighteenth century there were in every village of Malabar, various Nayar property groups, known as *taravads*, each under the legal guardianship of the oldest male member, or *karanavan*. For any individual, membership of a *taravad* was determined by descent through the female line, so the head of the household where one lived, that is, one's *karanavan*, was almost certain to be a maternal uncle, or great-uncle. As will be clear later, Nayar society was matrilinial.

Each *taravad* was linked to certain others, which were called *enangar*. Every few years all the girls in a *taravad* between the ages of about seven and twelve would be 'married' to men from their *enangar* in a ceremony known as *talikettukalyanam*, at which every 'husband' would tie a *tali*—a gold ornament—round the neck of his ritual bride. This would be followed by three days of seclusion together, after which the two need never see each other again. This 'marriage' was generally not consummated, but after it the bride had the social status of a mother and an adult woman. She also had to observe incest taboos in relation to men of her own *taravad*.

A woman married in the *tali*-ceremony would then receive lovers in her own home. They would arrive after supper and leave before breakfast. The first to come on any occasion had the right to stay the night, keeping others away by leaving his 'weapons' outside the door of the bed-chamber. In practice a woman would only have a few such lovers, and her relationship with each was known as *sambandham*. When she conceived a child, one, or sometimes more, of her lovers, would admit to paternity by making certain gifts of a recognized kind. This was essential for the child to be accepted as a legitimate member of the Nayar caste: at the same time it would become a member for life of its mother's *taravad*.

Primitive marriage, with its inevitable associations with the birth of children, ensures perpetuation of all the groups (as, for example, the Nayar *taravad*), of whatever size, which have a recognized part to play in any particular society. The more primitive the society, the more important this function of marriage will be. Now it could be, theoretically, the concern only of each individual group, and marriage as so far defined would allow even the smallest groups, right down to the extended family, to perpetuate themselves without looking outside to find marriage partners.

But no human society allows marriage or sexual relations between a man and a woman closely related to each other, save in quite exceptional circumstances. The forbidden degrees of kinship for marriage vary from one society to another: in English society, for example, every church has a notice stating them. In primitive societies the forbidden degrees are likely to extend much further. Most often they will not be symmetrical on both sides of the family, as ours are: this matter is tied up with the question of lineages, which has yet to be considered. But the rule of exogamy (marrying-out) as it is called, is universal in one form or other. (It corresponds to a prohibition on incest, or sexual relations with certain close kin, but the two are not necessarily of the same extent, and should definitely not be confused with each other.) Sometimes it is a question not so much of defining the group within which marriage is forbidden, as it is of prescribing some 'other' group within which the marriage partner must be found. The *enangar* of the Nayar provide an oblique instance of this in the *tali*-marriage. Some tribes, such as the Kariera of Australia, are divided into two halves, or moieties, such that a member of one must always marry a member of the other.[13] It is as if half the people in town were called Brown, and the other half Smith, with a rule that a Brown must always marry a Smith. And there are other structures which are yet more complicated.

Now marriage is so central an institution of society, that the rule of exogamy ensures that the different groups in any society must be in continuous relationship with each other. Whatever these groups may be, a marriage between any two of them is certain to affect their relationship with each other at the deepest level. It is not just a private matter between the two spouses; each of them will represent the group from which he or she comes, and these groups in turn will have various interests in the children born of the marriage, according to the custom of the particular society. Affinity, the relationship with others which is established through marriage ties, is thus a very important concept for primitive society.

Finally, it must be said that man is always dominant over woman: this is true individually and collectively. The husband rules the wife; the men in a family, or any other group, whether or not based on kinship, rule the women. So primitive society may be seen, at every level, as composed of a number of distinct groups, each controlled by its male members. The rule of exogamy makes certain that the groups are always in commerce with each other, and the primary articles of this commerce are women.[14] Primitive society is thus held together by the exchange of women between the different groups which comprise it. This is the rationale of primitive diplomacy. Sometimes compensation for the transfer of women is made by the movement of recognized valuable objects in the opposite direction. Such is the bride-price paid in cattle in a number of African tribes.[15] This emphasizes the essential 'economic' element in the marriage relationships which link different groups to each other.

Primitive marriage had therefore a wide-ranging social function which we must find difficult to appreciate. It is at one and the same time the institution which ensures the perpetuation of every socially significant group, and that which ensures that all such groups are continuously related to each other—if only indirectly—and in a way which is essentially beneficial to the whole society.

In our own society we see marriage in a quite opposite sense. We speak of the newly-married as setting up a 'home of their own' or as starting a 'new family'. We take it for granted that the married couple will be able to look after themselves from their own resources. To begin with they may have to live with one or other of the parents, but this is then regarded as an undesirable state to be brought to an end as soon as possible. The result is that marriage need hardly taken into account the interests of any but the parties to it. In so far as they are dependent on others—as all must be—this dependence will extend over a good part of the structure of the modern state. It is here that they will find opportunities for employment, and the living thereby provided. Much more important than any help or support from the extended family will be the various public services and welfare benefits which the modern state provides. These are much the same from one end of the country to the other. In our society, therefore, marriage can be regulated by such unpredictable and indefinable considerations as romantic love, and any young couple can leave their homes to start a new life together in the remotest corner of the world, if they are so inclined.

Even the birth of children hardly changes the position. Of course there is still need for parental responsibility, but there are many different agencies which care for children when the parents fail to do so. Indeed the modern state more or less requires parents to surrender their right to educate their own children, at least after a certain age. So the social function of primitive marriage, as this chapter describes it, is with us no more than a 'survival'. The implications of this, whether for the individual or society, have yet to be fully realized.

KINSHIP AND DESCENT

Kinship looms large among peoples who obtain their livelihood in small groups with simple tools. Among such peoples differences of aptitude and special training and duties do not, as in more complex societies, overwhelm the bonds between those who are born together and intermarry. The local groups within which personal relations are developed in work, rite and recreation are at the same time bodies of relatives who have ancestors in common and among whom a complex web of ties links every person with others throughout the community. The way in which comprehensive obligations of kinship direct the activities and relations which, in our society, are segregated out as more specifically political, economic and religious is a commonplace of social anthropology.[16]

Primitive society, as so far presented, would appear to consist of an indefinite (but probably very large) number of very small groups, inevitably related to each other by the operation of the rule of exogamy in each one of them, but with none able to carry on longer than a generation or so. In practice any society with so simple a structure would be unable to maintain itself over the course of time. For it would seem to be that a society containing no central or external institutions, whether social or economic, must create within itself a structure of inter-dependent social units, which must be more extensive and substantial than any form of domestic group. But how can this result be achieved, particularly where there is neither central government within the society itself, nor any other society upon which it depends?

Now among the hunters and gatherers[17]—people of the old stone age who in today's world are becoming more and more difficult to find—society is commonly organized into hordes, larger in size than the nuclear family, but with membership determined according to no definite social rule. The critical factor is much more the availability of the game and plants upon which survival depends. This is the case of the !Kung Bushmen of the Kalahari desert[18]—or perhaps the Mbuti pygmies of the Congo,[19] but significantly their economy is partly dependent on that of the surrounding Bantu tribes, who treat them almost as a class of servants.

By way of constrast we may look at the Negro society of Guyana: this is based on a constantly changing pattern of domestic groups, generally focused on a mother (or grandmother), at the head of the extended family, but here the men are employed in a modern mining and agricultural economy.[20]

But there is an enormous range of tribal societies, largely engaged in agriculture or husbandry, whose economy requires definite rules for the use and ownership of land or cattle, and for whom the Bushman solution of the problem of social organization at one extreme, or the Guyana solution at the other, would be wholly inadequate.

For these societies—which are the typical field of classical ethnography—there is a common solution to the problem, which is based upon a subtle adaptation of the rules of kinship. Now any people descended from a common ancestor are kin. In pre-literate societies, where the only possible recording device is the human memory (sometimes assisted, perhaps, by ancestor shrines), kinship is likely to be much more a social than a genetic concept. That is, people will be counted as kin, where this accords with local culture, even though they may not be related to each other by blood. This is called classificatory kinship. A classificatory brother, for instance, is a far nearer kinsman than an actual first cousin. So in talking of kinship, an anthropologist will always have in mind 'classificatory kinship'.[21]

In our own culture we acknowledge kinship equally through every possible line of ascent or descent, reckoning the closeness of the relationship only by the number of steps necessary to join the parties to it. So there is the same degree of kinship with one's maternal, as there is with one's paternal grandfather, or with one's daughter's daughter as there is with one's son's son. This is known as *cognatic*

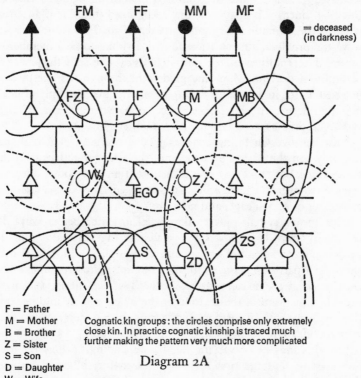

F = Father
M = Mother
B = Brother
Z = Sister
S = Son
D = Daughter
W = Wife

Cognatic kin groups: the circles comprise only extremely close kin. In practice cognatic kinship is traced much further making the pattern very much more complicated

Diagram 2A

kinship:[22] it is found in countless societies besides our own. The great objection to it is that it is essentially *ego*-centric: that is: *ego*, a typical individual member of the society, will share his kinship group with no other persons, except possibly his brothers and sisters. Since the primary social need of the primitive society is to establish a permanent social structure, the cognatic kinship group, inevitably changing with the life-cycle of its members, is of little use to it. There will also be almost unlimited overlapping, since every individual will be a member of every such group of all his kinsmen. This situation is like a ring fence, with a beam of light focused upon it, illuminating the living members of the society, and so moving on as one generation succeeds another.[23]

What is needed is a kinship structure with historical depth, and this leads to the concept of the lineage as a group of kin, who can actually demonstrate their descent from a common ancestor. Now if the descent is traced through both male and female forbears, one seems to get once more the confused pattern of cognatic kinship. But the lineage starts with the recognized founding ancestor, whereas the cognatic kin-group starts with ego. This alone does not solve the problem, since it leaves any individual to be a member of several different lineages. This difficulty is overcome by the principle of unilineal descent, which means descent through the line of only one sex. Thus, in a patrilineal system, one is a member only of one's father's lineage, and his father's and so on, where in a matrilineal system descent is traced through one's mother's line.[24]

Now the overwhelming advantage of a unilineal system is that not only can the basic corporate unit, the lineage, endure over the generations, but also every unit is distinct from every other one, and remains so over the generations. And every member of the society is a member of one lineage, and no more.

The lineage system may be developed in a number of ways. Its continuity may be ensured by providing that the succession to property, on the death of any member, takes place within it. A map showing a partition between lineages of the territory occupied by a tribe, such as the so-called 'tars' of the Tiv of Nigeria, may itself provide a diagram of the division of the whole society into its component lineages.[25] In mathematical terms the geometry of the map corresponds to the topology of the lineage structure.

Lineages may be of varying depths, depending on how far back one goes to find the first member. Indeed for different purposes lineages of varying degrees are recognized. The maximal lineage, based on the most distant recognized kinship, is the basic exogamous unit. The minimal lineage, in contrast, will be limited to those descended from the senior surviving member of it. It will naturally segment on his death, generally into as many minimal lineages as he will then have sons, with families of their own.

Segmentation at every level is undoubtedly a problem for the unilineal society, but it does not affect the basic operation of the lineage system. The lineages still endure, and they remain distinct from each other: there are just more of them than previously.[26] Provision is also made for the case of a lineage which becomes extinct.

The lineage principle is often extended so as to divide the whole society into different clans: the idea of the clan is that all its members are descended, patrilineally or matrilineally as the case may be, from the same mythical ancestor. At the level of the whole society there is often the same pattern of relationship between the clans as at the local level there is between the different lineages.

Now the lineages, and the clans also, work for the integration of the whole society, more particularly when descent is patrilineal. Marriage will invariably be between members of two different lineages, and each of them, as recognized corporations, will be involved in the preceding negotiations, and at the same have a continuing interest in the maintenance of the marriage tie. It is in this context that real significance of bride-price is to be seen: it is a pledge made by one corporation to another that a relationship established between them will be maintained.[27] It may well be renewed by successive 'preferred' marriages in succeeding generations.

A lineage does not necessarily have a geographical base: the Tiv may be the exception rather than the rule. Nuer lineages, of the Sudan, extend over the whole country, tending to unite different tribes (which are geographically based, but with their membership not based on common kinship), and which might otherwise be at odds.[28]

The Nuer, the Tiv and the Tallensi are patrilineal. This is not necessarily the more common case. But the matrilineal society does have problems which are of a quite different order, and which we cannot easily understand, since the bias of our own kinship system is patrilineal. One must not think of the matrilineal case as being a sort of mirror image of the patrilineal. In either case the women, needless to say, still bear the children, and the men still rule the women. The contrast between the two cases may be likened to that between King's and Queen's side openings in chess. Either gives a quite distinctive character to the game, but the rules themselves remain unchanged.

In the matrilineal society there is a built-in conflict between residence, kinship and marriage.[29] In case I the matrilineage keeps together: but the husband never resides with his wife. The Nayar case shows that this is not essential but then Nayar marriage is altogether exceptional; we must also recognize that our bias in favour of married couples living together is no more than a particular aspect of our own culture. In case II the men and women set up a matrimonial home, but then they are faced with the problem of integrating their children into the right matrilineage. For in this case the children are born into the residence group of their father's matri-

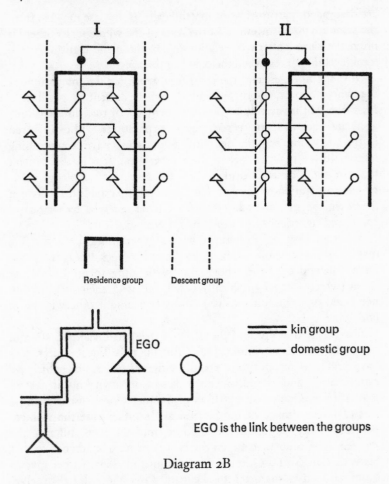

Diagram 2B

lineage, which can never be their own. The answer, surprising though it may be, is for the children, at adolescence, to move home to reside with their maternal uncles, as they do, for example, in the Trobriand islands.[30] This situation may give rise to continuous conflict, the kinship in a matrilineal society divides as often as it unites the different descent groups. This is far from meaning that the whole social purpose of lineage organization was lost: a 'matrilineal' society automatically incorporates the essential relationship between kin-groups and domestic groups.[31] Such a society may depend on more elaborate mechanisms for resolving conflict, which are the subject matter of Chapter 6.

Lineage provides for the segmentation of society, but at the same time the rule of exogamy, and the various different rules of residence and succession, ensure a working relationship between the different segments. There may be inherent conflict, but the segmentary society may always provide the 'legal' framework for its resolution. In practice this seems to be the lowest level of organization at which a wholly independent society—at least above the level of hunters and gatherers—may endure over the years.

3

Tribes without—and with—Rulers

THE LIMITS OF POLITICAL ORGANIZATION

This chapter is about politics in primitive societies. The subject is difficult to grasp, since the whole process of growing up in a modern Western society instils a concept of government which has no relation whatever to what is needed in a primitive community. We take for granted the existence of a central political authority, depending upon an extensive bureaucracy, and concerned in any number of different ways in the life of the people. It is difficult to conceive what the absence of government, in this sense, would mean. It is best to think for the moment of the services which a modern government provides, and to see why they are inherently beyond the reach of any primitive community. There can be no treasury in a nation without money; no department of education, where there is no writing; nor of transport, where all travel is on foot; nor of health, where there is no medical science. One is almost left to wonder whether political organization is necessary at all in primitive society: that is, does there need to be any structure of relationships, enforced by a common code of conduct, outside small local groups based on kinship? At first sight this may not seem to be needed for certain very primitive societies. The Australian aborigines, for example, used to live in small independent hordes, seldom having as many as a hundred members, which roamed across the empty desert, sustaining themselves by hunting and gathering, subject to no authority but that exercised by the old men in the group. Even so these hordes came together every year for their most important religious ceremonies, and in these meetings (which were essential also for the exchange of wives) a different pattern of authority did prevail, and it did not depend only on recognized ties of kinship.[1]

A primitive people requires a political structure which extends across its whole society, to provide for some degree of unity and co-ordination of its activities. This does not necessarily demand centralized authority, administrative machinery or formal judicial institutions, in which the distribution of power will be reflected in differences of wealth, privilege or status, as it is in our society. Countless primitive societies lack such institutions: these may be regarded as stateless rather than anarchical. At the same time primitive economy hardly allows for such status symbols as we normally associate with the possession of power and authority.

The whole difference between a state with a centralized government, and a stateless society, may be one more of ideology than anything else. This is well illustrated by Leach's study of the Kachin tribes of Burma.[2] These tribes seem to have two alternative systems of government, known as Gumsa and Gumlao. Gumsa is centralized and hierarchical; Gumlao is stateless and egalitarian. But neither system is in equilibrium, and the whole point of the study is to show how one can be transformed into the other, without the day to day life of the tribe being much affected. However, such imbalance is far from characteristic of every primitive society. The two contrasting categories of the stateless society, and the unitary state, provide the best starting point for any study, although there are certainly intermediate types of political organization.

THE STATELESS SOCIETY

The problem in the stateless society is to provide for a political structure which will co-ordinate all the different recognized groups. We have already seen that the largest group based solely on kinship —that is, in the sense of a blood relationship which can be traced through identifiable individuals—is extremely small. Even where kinship is traced through several degrees, say through the male line, the largest possible group is unlikely to exceed a hundred members, of whom the most distantly related may be no more than sixth or seventh cousins. The average kin-group will probably be much smaller. In a population of 200,000, which is not particularly large, this would be far too small a social unit to be the basis of any workable political structure extending across the whole of the society. One answer—particularly characteristic of parts of Africa—is to extend the lineage principle beyond the degrees of traceable kinship, so as to constitute the 'clan', in the way already explained in Chapter 2.[3]

The whole political structure of a society may then be developed so as to depend entirely on the interaction of larger and larger units based on the principle of common descent each comprising a number

of comparable units of lower degree. The rules for the interrelationship of the different units, at whatever level, will be an important
part of the common culture of the whole society. Between any two
units, which are together comprised in a unit of higher degree, there
will be both conflict and harmony. Conflict will arise over any matter
in which a wrong is seen as having been inflicted by a member of one
unit on a member of the other: there will be harmony where two or
more related units must act together against another unit of higher
degree, which in the same way has harmed one of their common
members. Now there may well be a limit to the consolidation of
related units for the purposes of joint action; beyond this limit
political co-ordination will be impossible, except perhaps for the
intermittent waging of war against a neighbouring people. So also,
below a certain level there will be no recognized scope for conflict:
any dispute, even if arising out of so grave a matter as homicide,
will be resolved by arbitration within the group, leading to an
imposed solution. For example, if a Nuer tribesman kills his brother,
the imposed solution will be for him to marry the brother's widow,
where the result of his killing a distant cousin would be a blood-feud
between the two largest separate kinship groups of which they were
both members, only to be abated by the need for common action by
these two groups against some yet larger outside group. This tension
between conflict and common action is critical in the political structure of any primitive society.[4]

So far the political structure of the stateless society has been
looked at in a rather abstract way. This is represented in the diagram
above.[5] Here at level 4, E, a minimal group, may be in conflict
with F or G, over one question, yet united with them, within group
C, at level 3, to pursue a conflict against group D. The origins of this
conflict may lie in a dispute between groups F and H at level 4, but
since F and H are not within the same groups at level 3, it is at this
level that the conflict between them must be resolved. The rules of

conduct will vary at each successive level, with an increasing tendency at the lower levels towards enforced arbitration, and at the higher level towards the use of violence. There is a modern parallel in gang warfare in New York.[6]

This type of structure is known as *segmentary*, for obvious reasons. In many African societies the segments, at whatever level, are organized on the principle of lineage, which as Chapter 2 showed, has the advantage of determining uniquely the appropriate membership for every individual in the society. This is not essential: the political organization of the Nyakyusa of Tanzania, for example, is based on age-sets whose interaction provides a different kind of government.[7]

Assuming a lineage based political organization, the question then arises as to whether it needs to be reinforced by any other structure. The general answer is that it must be so: lineage alone provides a cloth with a warp but no weft. One way to reinforce the lineage structure is to duplicate it in some other institution of the society, such as its system of land tenure or its religion.

The first means is adopted by the Tiv of Nigeria.[8] These are an interesting people, because although not far short of a million in number, they regard themselves as all being members of a single maximal lineage, descended from one common ancestor, eighteen generations back, called Tiv. Their common genealogical structure is reflected in the territorial allocation of their land for cultivation. The relationship between the different lineage groups—essential to the unity of the people—is then maintained by commerce in the different produce of the land at the local markets which exist throughout the country.[9]

The Tallensi of Northern Ghana maintain a very well-developed system of inter-related clans and lineages by means of an elaborate ancestor cult. This depends upon every clan and lineage being tied to a particular territory, which provides the sites of the appropriate ancestor shrines. At each of these shrines there is a prescribed pattern of sacrifice, which incorporates very precise rules as to what parts are to be played, and by whom, on any particular occasion. The important point is that certain participants will represent other clans and lineages. So the ancestor shrines for the Tallensi play the same part as the markets do for the Tiv.[10]

Whereas the lineage structure of the Tiv and the Tallensi is in each case inherent in their system of land tenure, that of the Nuer cuts right across it. The Nuer territorial unit is the tribe, which is economically self-sufficient, and is the largest effective social group. The population of the tribe is relatively large, and so it is sub-divided through various degrees into tribal segments, each of which is a tribe in miniature. Every tribe recognizes a dominant or aristocratic clan, but since any one clan extends throughout the country, the majority

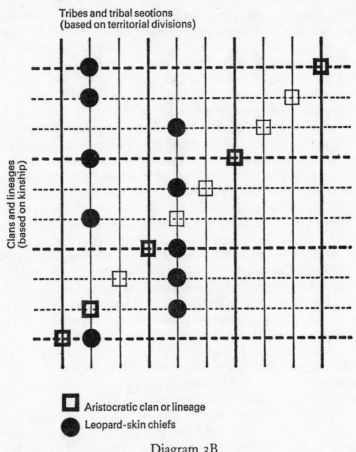

Diagram 3B

of its members will not be aristocrats: indeed there are clans which are nowhere dominant. This hardly affects their welfare. The question is not one of power, wealth or privilege: it is no more than that the lineage structure of the dominant clan provides a kinship basis for the political organization of the tribe.[11] The relationship of Nuer clans and tribes is illustrated by Diagram 3B.

The stateless society has very definite social limitations. It is inevitably far too egalitarian for any but the most primitive economic activity. There can be very little differentiation of roles except on the basis of age and sex. The Nuer do have special functionaries, known as leopard-skin chiefs, who have a definite role to play in the settlement of certain disputes. The officials of the different Tallensi shrines or Tiv market chiefs may play a similar part: all of these offices are likely to be found in certain prescribed lineages. But these societies have practically no power to adapt to unforeseen circumstances, such as the immigration of people of quite different cultures, or the imposition of colonial rule. The Nuer have absorbed a number of Dinka, but the Dinka, who are their neighbours, and are alike in culture, can only be assimilated by being adopted as members of the different Nuer tribes and clans.[12] But the absence of central authority means that there is no real possibility of any sort of foreign policy. The stateless society lives on a sort of social frontier. So long as there is no need (or compulsion) to develop its economy, or to adapt to an alien culture, it can maintain its political structure. But this is hardly the condition of any part of the modern world, however remote from the centres of Western civilization.

STATEHOOD AND AUTHORITY

The stateless society may be seen as held together by a network of ties, which provides for the necessary regulations of the lives of the people, and which may be compared to a woven cloth in which every strand has essentially the same function. The picture is abstract: what it portrays is social, in the sense of being made up exclusively of different types of human relationship recognized and maintained by a society. Now upon this network of ties there may be superimposed another, characteristically focused on a central point of *authority*. It is as if a spider's web were to be laid above the woven cloth. And the spider at the centre will gradually be a single individual, whose social role is quite explicitly distinct from that of any other member of his 'state'. This individual will be the 'chief' or 'king' of his people: the actual part allocated to him will vary greatly from one culture to another, and it is very difficult to make useful generalizations about the institutions of 'high office' in primitive society. There is, however, a sort of ascending scale of effective chiefly control of the day to day interests of the people. Progressing from one society to another, one may see how this control is intensified, and comes to affect more and more the life and welfare of the people. The further one gets up the scale, the more one will find points of tension, generally focused on certain recognized officials, between the centralized administration of the chief, and the underlying social structure of the society. In such officials we may recognize a classic case of role conflict, such as in our own society we may find in the conflict between a man's duty to his employer, and his duty to his family.

A good person to represent the lowest point on the scale is the Reth, or King, of the Shilluk, another people of the Southern Sudan.[13] Now the Reth is not at the head of any centralized administration: politically the Shilluk are almost stateless, like their neighbours, the Nuer and the Dinka. The Reth's authority is spiritual. The welfare of the people depends directly on his own state of health. He is a sort of high-priest, with power to mediate with supernatural powers for success in war, or for rain. He is seen as the successor of the first mythical king, called Nyikang, and so represents the power which creates and maintains the cosmos. The Reth, therefore, is the idealized source of Shilluk social order, and this function he fulfils merely by existing.

To the South of the Shilluk, in the border country of Uganda and Zaire, one finds the Alur,[14] who are known for their particular type of chiefship. This is more advanced than that of the Shilluk. The Alur *chiefs* still have no bureaucratic apparatus, but in addition to the common chiefly power to call for rain, they have a recognized judicial authority, which they may exercise by going on circuit round their chiefdoms. It is a common obligation of chiefs always to be accessible to their people for the settling of disputes. This definitely makes for stability in the community, and it is significant that the rule of Alur chiefs has been extended over neighbouring people as much by invitation as by conquest. Now the position of an Alur chief is maintained by the payment of tribute and fines—a very common practice in the primitive state. Sometimes the tribute is in terms of service, consisting of work on the chief's farms. None of this means any acquisition or accumulation of wealth by the chief: the Alur economy has no money, nor any means of saving or investment. The tribute brought to a chief must almost immediately be disposed of by him, generally by means such as will enhance his authority, say, by customary gifts to subordinate chieflets, or by holding a ceremonial feast for all the local people.

The Alur state, with its various chiefs (but no king at the centre), demonstrates a special political capacity beyond the scope of the stateless society: it has absorbed, on varying terms neighbouring peoples of markedly different culture. For inherent in the centralized government of a chief is the idea of class-differentiation, with different powers and roles being assigned at various levels of the hierarchy. Once this principle is accepted, it may be almost indefinitely extended, so as to provide for a political structure in which many diverse communities and interests may be incorporated. One example of this is to be found in the kingdom of Ankole,[15] to the South of the Alur, which was divided into two quite distinct sections, the one dominating the other. The first, whose members were called Bahima, naturally included the royal line, and were pastoralists. The second group, BaIru, were agriculturalists, and were in every way subordinate: they provided as tribute the whole needs of the court for agricultural produce—including beer! The neighbouring kingdom of Ruanda[16] extended this socially differentiated structure to include a third group, a pygmy type people known as Twa, who were traditionally hunters and potters. One is almost inclined to see the beginnings of something like the Indian caste system, itself an important subject for anthropological study, but beyond the scope of this book.

At the level of the state ruled by a king, such as is reached by Ankole and Ruanda—and by many other peoples in this part of Africa round the great lakes—it is essential if the king's rule is to be effective throughout the land, for there to be a fairly elaborate administrative structure. This will have both territorial and central components. The king, at least to govern his most distant territories, must rely on subordinate chiefs, who in practice will have their own comparable administrations, but on a lesser scale. The appointment of chiefs is often a great problem; they will be tempted to usurp, and there will be present all the conflicts which Shakespeare portrays in his historical plays. This difficulty may be overcome by a political system such as that of the Bemba of Zambia, in which, although the principal district chiefs are members of the royal family, the chieftainships have a recognized order of precedence, leading in the end to the position of paramount chief of the whole people.[17]

The alternative is to appoint a new chief entirely on personal merit. This was the rule in Buganda,[18] the greatest of all the kingdoms round the great lakes. But a local chief appointed in this way will always be tempted to use the authority inevitably delegated to him so as to establish the chiefly prerogative of his own line: indeed this is often a sort of half-way stage between the two principles.

That is, the local chiefships may be hereditary, but not in any recognized royal line.

The central administration—or 'court'—of a king is likely to be very complex: this is because it must serve a number of different purposes. The first may be to establish, definitely, the king's status in the eyes of the people. He will therefore, in the shape of his palace, have a home far more extensive and imposing than that of any of his subjects. He will also have a much greater number of wives and servants, who, incidentally, by being chosen from different parts of the realm, will play an important part in maintaining his authority. A local chief's loyalty will be more certain if his daughter is one of the royal wives: this principle often extends to bringing to court other members of chiefs' families, such as their sons, almost as hostages for their fathers' good behaviour.

In addition to the retinue of wives, servants, pages and so, a king will have a number of special officials in his own household, whose roles will extend in practice to the definite participation in the government of the kingdom. The Katikiro, in Buganda, for example, although in theory the head of the Kabaka's—the king's —household, was in practice the prime minister. Even in England, today, certain officials of the royal household are appointed to exercise political authority. In Buganda also, the mother of Kabaka, and a chosen sister, but, note, not any of his wives, had special privileges and authority.

A special line of craftsmen, such as Iru blacksmiths in Ankole, is often attached to the court.[19] Blacksmiths are an important case, since they alone can make weapons out of iron, and the security of the court requires the exclusive control of this power.

The court may carry out its territorial administration with the aid of a council, generally recruited from the senior chiefs—such, originally, was the English Privy Council. At the same time there will be royal messengers going to and fro all parts of the Kingdom, as part of the machinery for co-ordinating the King's rule.

Finally, there is the crisis of succession in the royal line. Nothing is more important to the well-being of a primitive kingdom, than that it should be united under a strong king. This will not be one who is old or ill in health. This means, not surprisingly, a high rate of royal mortality, even to the point of the ritual killing of an ailing or weakening sovereign. Sir James Frazer, in his classic work, 'The Golden Bough',[20] tried to establish that a primitive ruler, with quasi-divine status, could never be allowed a natural death. Frazer's scholarship may now be discredited, but undoubtedly the unique ritual status of the primitive ruler made his death the gravest possible crisis for his subjects, and one inevitably deepened by the absence of any definite order of succession. There could be any number of princes equally entitled to succeed, especially with the proliferation of royal wives. In Ankole the rival claimants would lead their supporters into a civil war, ending only with the death or banishment of all but one, who would then become the Mugabe, or king.[21] In Buganda, the court included a special chief, the Kasuju, who took charge of the princes, and regulated the succession on the death of the Kabaka, with the named successor being then approved by the Katikiro and the ten senior chiefs.[22] Even so, the Kabaka might still execute his brothers (or in practice, half-brothers), to prevent their usurping him. These primitive peoples seem continually to be re-fighting the Wars of the Roses—which took place in England in the fifteenth century—and for much the same political reasons.

BUREAUCRACY, THE MODERN STATE
AND THE ALTERNATIVE SOCIETY

The previous section, on 'statehood and authority', has the great fascination of seeming to portray a type of government found in Europe until times so recent that many traces of it still survive, particularly in England. There, at 'Hampton Court', a former royal palace, free homes—of great comfort and elegance—are still given by the Crown to a select few who have rendered notable public service. This is almost the sort of reward that a Kabaka or Mugabe might bestow on a favoured official, ensuring at the same time his continued stay at court. In England, or elsewhere in the modern world, this sort of institution is known to be no more than a survival, not in any way representing the true nature of contemporary political institutions.

The modern state is characterized by quite different organizational structures, all of which are different aspects of bureaucracy. The use of the word 'bureaucracy' in political analysis derives largely from the work of Max Weber (1864–1920), one of the founding fathers of modern social science. Weber saw bureaucracy primarily as characterizing the machinery of state government, and historically this is where it first developed. With the growth of the modern corporate state, in which many kinds of strictly non-governmental enterprises inevitably exist on the scale and at the level of complexity of state government, the bureaucratic model becomes much more widely applicable. Indeed, many of the giant industrial and commercial concerns of the Western world, which are nominally independent of national governments (as they would never be in a Marxist state), are far greater, in economic terms, than many nations of the third world—where, significantly, the bureaucratic model is much less appropriate (although such nations almost all purport to adopt it).[23]

What then are the characteristics of bureaucratic government? According to Weber, it is carried on continuously, by properly authorized officials, each with a prescribed, but limited area of responsibility, to which appointment is made by officials at a higher level (thus importing an essentially hierarchical structure), on the basis of recognized and appropriate skills, with remuneration according to an agreed salary, and with no power, on the part of the official himself, to dispose of his office, or any of its benefits.[24]

The use of writing underlies any bureaucratic system.[25] Not only is the whole operation based on written records, but the underlying structure, or in legal terms, constitution is contained in written documents. These take the place of the validation of power structures, in terms of oral tradition, which characterize the political systems considered in the earlier sections of this chapter. In legal terms the basis of the constitution is legislative,[26] and in practice it is largely the bureaucrats themselves, that is, those whose occupations derive their whole character and authority from the constitution, who have the power to modify it. This, at first sight, contradicts the principle of representative and elective government—at least on the legislative side—which applies, nominally at least, in many bureaucratic states, until it is seen that the elected legislators are themselves part of the bureaucracy, distinguishable from their fellow bureaucrats in terms of function and appointment, but none the less, of essentially the same kind.

Bureaucracy was an inevitable development of the industrial revolution, which required the organization of man-power on an unprecedented scale, together with the development of a vast number of special skills. The complexity of the resulting order soon demanded its own skills, administrative rather than political. At the same time the face-to-face contacts characteristic of the political life of the pre-industrial state became much less important as the systematic use of written rules, and the recording of written agreements, could be turned to govern all human relationships. Just as the workman in the factory came to be alienated, in Marxist terms,[27] from the ultimate product to which his labour contributed, so also, in his relationship with those who governed him, he found himself dealing with an official allowed only to deal according to prescribed written rules. This, of course, made the identity of the official quite unimportant, and in a later development apt to be superseded by a purely mechanical contrivance. (Thus, originally, all telephone calls had to be connected by a human operator; now almost all are connected automatically. In purely bureaucratic terms the change is somewhat superficial, since telephone operators were always trained to operate, *automatically*, according to prescribed written rules. So long as the human element was present, the rules might actually be disregarded. The basic automatic telephone exchange was invented by a Kansas City undertaker, who was angry because the local switchboard operator favoured one of his business rivals.)

At a certain level, in any bureaucracy, the exercise of power requires decisions of policy, not prescribed by the rule-book, but such decisions tend to be restricted to a high level. All the multiplicity of bureaucratic functions which have no room for such discretion are apt to be superseded by automatic equipment, of which the manual switchboard operators provide but one example. This parallels the superseding of domestic crafts, notably weaving and spinning, by the textile mills of the industrial revolution.

Weber was convinced that bureaucracy was the only possible form of government for the modern state, but he appreciated that its defects would lead many to work for the adoption of alternatives to it. One common reaction is to corrupt the system itself, which means finding an official who can be dealt with as an individual, and not according to the rule book. Essentially this is a regression to earlier traditional forms of government, because very quickly those bureaucratic functions which combine incentive and opportunity for corruption tend to be valued for these attributes, and to be allocated not according to the rule-book, but on the basis of the right informal, and always personal contacts. A position can quickly be reached, where the allocation and exercise of these functions depends on an informal (and needless to say, unwritten) tradition.[28] The consequence is a loss of bureaucratic efficiency and impartiality, but it must be recognized that these are pre-eminently bureaucratic values.

Bureaucracy above all assigns roles according to skills acquired within institutions which it itself maintains. Those concerned in education—in its widest sense—are the most important. It follows that little or no provision is made for those who fail to acquire such skills. The drop-out is a characteristic figure of the bureaucratic society. To some extent the system corrects this defect in itself, by incorporating means of looking after those who fail according to its norms, by providing in the first instance welfare benefits, and as a last resort, prisons, mental hospitals and other correctional institutions.

At the same time bureaucracy is now counteracting its own facelessness by providing increasing numbers of social workers, whose case-load is always worked through on a face-to-face basis. In the end corruption, welfare, social case-work still fail to modify bureaucracy sufficiently for it to answer to the needs of all of those it should care for—which is indeed the total population. The diversity of human kind in the modern industrial state goes far beyond the provisions of the bureaucratic rule-book. Inevitably there are categories which are left out, and some of them become organized groups,[29] which create their own political systems in disregard of the overpowering bureaucracy. But it is not of the nature of the bureaucratic state to tolerate such groups, particularly those whose numbers use violence to undermine the security which, ideally, it provides. According to purely bureaucratic values the merit in putting a member of a New York street gang[30] in a correctional institution, is that that is part of the bureaucratic system, while the gang is not. The fact that the gang, and the social milieu from which it springs, was never consulted about these values (often thought of under the heads of 'law and order'), is not considered relevant.

In the end bureaucracy can tolerate no alternatives. However much it must, on any terms, do its best to suppress the violence of the street gang, it is bound to threaten also the essential peacefulness of a group such as the Pennsylvania Dutch, who wish to be an alternative society, for purely religious reasons. The technology which is both the hand-maid and the justification of modern bureaucracy will almost certainly develop in such a way as to accentuate the defects of the system, at the same time providing more refined means for suppressing, rather than curing, them. The alternative societies may sometimes terrify us, but if Weber was right, and bureaucracy is now the only alternative to them, we may well wonder at the price to be paid for progress .

4

Human Kind and Natural Resources

The possibility of life for any species depends entirely on the physical circumstances around it. Every known species is more or less specific in this sense. In the right environment it can sustain the life of its members: this is how the habitat of the species is defined. But outside it there will be little or no chance of survival.[1]

Within its habitat all that a species needs for life is provided by nature. This does not mean that any one species will consume all the natural products within its habitat: the habitats of any number of different species can well co-exist within a given geographical area. The common structure is for a number of parallel series of successive higher forms of life to exist side by side. At the lowest level of organic life, at least on dry land, there must be at least some form of plant growth. In deserts, mountains and polar regions where there is no such growth, there is no other form of life. But even the most limited plant cover will in its turn sustain some range of insects, reptiles, birds or mammals, all adapted not only to the foodstuffs which the plants provide, but also to the climate in which they grow. The more exuberant the plant cover, the greater is the range of other life which it supports. The extreme example of this is the complex of life which exists in a tropical rain forest, where typically one plant may be capable of growth only as a parasite on another, and every species of bird will depend on a narrow range of plant or insect life, with the animal population selectively exploiting the whole range of organic species, including—for the carnivores—other animals in the environment. In all this there is something which can be called 'economy', in the sense that every species finds in its own habitat resources which it can, indeed must, exploit for its own survival. More than this, the members of the species must compete for these resources, a critical fact in determining the size of the total population. An event, whether natural, such as a flood, a drought, or an epidemic, or caused by man, such as the construction of a reservoir,[2] which affects the environment, will change the habitats of the species present, and some will gain from it and others lose. Few species ever destroy their own habitat: some cataclysmic event may do this, in whole or in part, but that is a different matter. In such an event the population is reduced, even to the point of extinction. In contrast, where a species finds a new habitat—as rabbits did when they were introduced to Australia —its population will increase so as to exploit fully the new resources available. In this process other species—present earlier on the scene —may in turn find their habitats reduced, or even their own kind wantonly destroyed. Significantly this latter event is almost always brought about, indirectly it may be, by man: carnivorous animals never efface the other animal species on which they prey, for this would be destroying their own habitat. The balance is always maintained. But the goats brought by settlers to the Galapagos Islands are rapidly destroying the habitat of other earlier, and much rarer species, which cannot compete with them.

Man's treatment of his natural environment is a complete contrast to that of any form of animal life. His need for food is generalized, not specific, which means that a human community can adapt to an astonishingly wide range of possible living places. There is an almost endless list of natural products consumed by man as food,[3] and from it an equally unlimited variety of different possible diets can be compiled. So long as the components of any such diet are present in a given area, then it can provide the home for a human community. In theory all that is needed is a minimum balanced diet, that is one in which every component has an essential nutritive role, and is available in the quantities necessary to play that role. The scientific research done into the food values that such a diet must contain is only of indirect interest to the anthropologist. In practice all human diets contain a super-abundance of some components, including at the same time, if only on special occasions, others which are inessential.

There are good reasons for this. The degree of social organization necessary for a human community, combined with the relatively long average life of its individual members, demands an exceptionally dependable habitat. It is the *bad years* in a given environment which decide whether men can live in it, and in what numbers. It is significant therefore that a tribe of primitive hunter-gatherers, such as the !Kung Bushmen of Botswana, never want for the Mongongo nuts, which constitute the most important element in their diet.[4] Indeed their habitat invariably provides these in quantities far greater than actually needed. At the same time they are but one of eighty-four plant species which comprise their diet throughout the year, showing, even for so primitive and isolated a group, and one confined to an exceptionally barren environment, a range of consumption several times greater than that of any animal species, even one in so profligate an environment as a tropical rain-forest.

The food gathered by the !Kung Bushmen requires some preparation before it is eaten. This is an example of the fact that organization and technology, at however primitive a level, is essential for meeting the material needs of any human community. This fact, combined with the need for super-abundant resources, gives rise to the uniquely human institution of leisure. This can be defined as any combined use of time and resources for purposes other than pure material subsistence. There may not be much choice open to the individual as to how his share of available leisure should be used. Indeed the whole lesson of cultural anthropology is that individual and community use of leisure is determined by traditional norms, and may well consist of activities more commonly thought of under the heads of religion or politics. Leisure is, however, occasionally devoted to economic enterprise, to the point even of complete innovation. This, although a rare, indeed if not unknown, use of leisure among peoples such as the !Kung Bushmen, is one which is taken for granted in any modern community. Leisure may also be used counter-productively, not only by twentieth-century millionaires who squander their wealth in Las Vegas or Monte Carlo, but by twentieth-century hunters and gatherers such as the Hadza of Tanzania, who willingly risk losing their metal-headed arrow-heads, which are essential for big-game hunting, in a pure game of chance to which they are all addicted.[5] (It need hardly be said that this activity does not deprive anyone of *essential* foodstuffs: big-game is marginal in the Hadza diet.)

ECOLOGY AND THE ORGANIZATION OF LIFE

Ecology is most generally defined as the interaction of an organism with its environment. The word has now acquired a highly emotive content, because its meaning has become focused on one particular organism, human society, and one particular environment, the world, and at the present moment the interaction between the two threatens the well-being of both of them. How this may be is a matter for the last section in a chapter on economic anthropology, and not the first.

The relevant organism in any specific ecological context may be only one member of a species, or it may extend to all the members of a number of different species living in community with each other. In the human context the social scientist will focus on a particular human population, defined by some common characteristic, often territorial, which sets it apart from other such populations. But before looking at any cases of human ecology, or indeed at any ecological situations where a human community plays a significant part, it is best to see what happens in purely natural circumstances. Here it is convenient to start with the representatives of a recognized species present in the environment which is being studied. One can take, for instance, the chimpanzees in the Gombe Stream Reserve in Uganda.[6] For them the environment will consist not only of geophysical factors, such as soil and climate, but biological factors such as all the other species present happen to comprise. The size and life-style of the chimpanzee population will depend on all these factors, some of which will be specific to this particular environment. (The chimpanzees there have certain items of diet, such as ants and termites, which they do not eat elsewhere.) The chimpanzees will occupy a niche in a generalized eco-system. Their occupation will be dynamic in the sense of having a significant effect on other species present, for whom, indeed the chimpanzees, in turn will form a part of the environment.

In general a natural eco-system is in a state of dynamic equilibrium. Change, over the short term, is inherent in any organic system, but so also is the tendency always to restore the balance. The individual chimpanzee dies, but the population, and its profile, are maintained within surprisingly narrow limits. It might be that the Gombe chimpanzees would go on the rampage, and reduce the habitats of competing species to their own advantage, and thus see their population increase, to establish a new, and different equilibrium, but this hypothesis pre-supposes a degree of aggression ·beyond the chimpanzee norm, and there is no scientific justification for this. (Some aggression, of course, such as that of a carnivorous species, is a common aspect of stable eco-systems.) Equally, the chimpanzees might succumb to some terrible epidemic, and the competing species fill up the ecological space thus made available. But again the presence of pathogens and the incidence of disease are inherent in a stable eco-system.

A natural eco-system tends not only to be stable, but also to reach a climax: that is, the interaction of the different species present is such as to generate the maximum amount of organic productivity.[7] This suggests a primeval world made up of any number of eco-systems, each specific according to geophysical factors, but all existing, and continuing to exist, in a state of climax equilibrium.

But what is the place of man? This question must be answered in a number of stages. In the first stage man must be assumed to have no command over his environment other than which follows from a society organized to hunt the game and gather the plants occurring in nature, and prepare them for its own consumption. Even at this stage the very presence of the species, man, makes it a component of the existing eco-system. It may, however, not be a significant component, in that such communities never exploit all the resources which they need. That is, the !Kung Bushmen, for example, are able to preserve their traditional way of life, precisely because they never eat all the Mongongo nuts available. The rest of the eco-system of which they are a part would be little changed by their disappearance. Indeed it can, in contrast, tolerate the presence of human kind in significantly larger numbers, as happens when Bantu pastoralists, who are neighbours to the !Kung, are forced to become guests in !Kung territory in times of drought and famine, catastrophes which never threaten the !Kung way of life.[8] So at the natural level man is a sort of ecological epiphenomenon. This explains why the anthropologists, R. B. Lee and I. Devore, are able to write that

> Cultural man has been on earth for some 2,000,000 years; for over 99 per cent of this time he has lived as a hunter-gatherer . . . the hunting way of life has been the most successful and persistent adaptation man has ever achieved.[9]

One reason why man so long remained a hunter-gatherer is that a geo-political solution could always be found to economic problems. Long before essential resources became short in any given area, a part of its population could migrate to another where they were still abundant. For man it never mattered that the migration was to an eco-system of an entirely different character, for this could always be dealt with by an adaptation of diet. In some new areas there might be an unprecedented need for clothing, heat or shelter, but these too were within man's range long before anyone had any other life but that of a hunter or gatherer. Successive adaptations therefore created an incredible spectrum of economic subsistence, ranging from people such as the Netsilik Eskimos of the far north of Canada, whose entire livelihood depends on the exploitation of caribou in summer and seals in winter, in an astonishingly simple eco-system,[10] to the Mbuti pygmies of north-east Zaire, who inhabit the vastly complex and luxuriant eco-system of the tropical rain-forest.[11] The key characteristic of all these people is that although they adapted themselves, they never adapted their environments. This in the end proved fatal to their way of life. Its critical limitation was that it could support only very low population densities, and if man was to multiply even to a fraction of his present population, some radical new adaptation of his environment had to take place. This is why the advent of agriculture and herding is the most extraordinary and significant revolution in the history of man.

The strictly economic and social consequences of this revolution are considered in Chapter 5. Its ecological consequences, which are just as critical, are considered here. In ecological terms the same insight lies behind both agriculture and herding. It is that if circumstances could be contrived to favour the growth of particular natural species, whether of plants or animals, on which man can subsist most profitably, then a given territory could support a far higher population, and sustain, indeed require, entirely new types of human institutions. Agriculture, because of its relatively fixed base, provides a better illustration of how this happens, than herding.

The idea behind agriculture is to select a certain plant species, and then to create the conditions favourable to its growth within the confines of a narrow space, at the same time preventing the growth of competing species. At the most elementary level, such as with a vegetative root-crop, like the familiar potato, this result might be achieved, in the right soil and climate, simply by uprooting all competing plant species, and fencing the cultivated area to protect it from hostile animals. At the more advanced level of seed crops, such as all cereals, the seed must be sown in specially prepared ground, at the right time of year, and the weeding carried out much more intensively. Indeed the *natural* conditions in which such crops grow with sufficient abundance to be useful for human subsistence occur so rarely on the face of the earth, and in regions so little attractive to hunters and gatherers, that it is often thought that these factors explain why the agricultural revolution occurred so late in human history.[12] But once the revolution did occur, cultivation was confined but for a moment to such marginal regions, and then spread rapidly throughout the whole world. There was not necessarily a single integrated diffusion process, but however this may be, the advantages of agriculture, wherever it was possible, appeared quite overwhelming to human kind. That is why the Lacandon Indians in the tropical rain-forest of southern Mexico, who live in an exceptionally abundant natural eco-system, still prefer to subsist by the cultivation of maize, a uniquely unsuitable crop for the region.[13] Hunters and gatherers now survive mostly in areas utterly unsuited for herding or agriculture, like the near desert inhabited by the !Kung Bushmen or the Arctic wastes which are the home of the Netsilik Eskimos.

The ecology of agriculture may be illustrated by a typical maize-growing community of middle America, such as the Chamula of southern Mexico.[14] Maize shows one particular consequence of agriculture, which is the conscious adaptation, by breeding, of a plant species, so as to make it particularly suitable for intensive cultivation in a given region. No natural grass could possibly produce such food values as does the highly developed strain of maize sown in the Chamula highlands. (There is in fact no certainty about the *natural* origins of maize.)[15] The simple cultivation of maize, from the selection of ears from the previous harvest, through the whole cycle of planting, weeding, harvesting, threshing and storing, requires the constant attention of a population which is large in relation to the size of the cultivated area, a factor which imports an immediate risk of disaster, following any crop failure. At the same time, a people such as the Chamulas, will have an attitude to their maize, quite different to that of the !Kung Bushmen to their Mongongo nuts. Every ear of maize produced will be consumed; indeed there will be a direct relation between the number of consumers and the number of producers. So the Chamula, far from being an epiphenomenon in a generalized natural eco-system, will be the controlling factor in a highly artificial eco-system. The problems of political and social organization which this involves are dealt with in Chapter 5. The purely ecological consequences are by no means exhausted. The concentrated growth of an artificial strain of maize in a prepared environment not only exhausts the soil in a way not found in natural grass-lands, but allows secondary organisms to flourish at a level which they would never achieve in a natural eco-system. The first factor can be dealt with by crop-rotation, but since cultivation encourages population growth, in the end there will be an irresistible tendency to rotate over too short a period of time, to the permanent exhaustion of the soil, as can be seen in many parts of Chamula today. The second factor encourages not only *pathogens* which cause plant disease and crop failure, but vermin, such as the mice and rats which plague the Chamula, which can deplete the harvest.

This is not the end of the story. The density of an agricultural population encourages the spread of epidemic diseases (although on nothing like the scale of the urban epidemics of medieval Europe), while at the same time reliance on a single crop can lead to diseases caused by a deficiency in the food values not found in it. Chronic deficiency diseases such as *kwashiorkor* are scarcely found among hunters and gatherers.[16] The natural stability of which they have the advantage is to be contrasted with the characteristic instability which is the sort of retribution which nature takes on cultivators. None the less stability is an almost universal human ideal, and the so-called homeostatic institutions of society exist not only to maintain it, but to do so in the face of hostile and unpredictable natural forces. A balance which is destroyed in nature (however unintentionally) is to be restored by culture. This is a starting point for all economic anthropology. One measure is out of the question: the clock cannot be put back. The world of hunters and gatherers had a *total* population of 10,000,000 people.[17] The estimate may be a little bit out, and the natural resources of the world might well have maintained a greater population at this level. They would never have been enough for a population some three- or four-hundred times greater, and that is the size of the problem. We can envy the !Kung Bushmen: we cannot imitate them.

SURPLUS AND INVOLUTION

Economic surplus is one of the most debated of all topics in the social sciences. The questions which are asked are: Does it exist at all?[18] If so, how is it, or should it be, measured? How is it, or should it be allocated? These questions are much too tendentious, and much too general. Another question (which can be asked of almost any society) provides a much better starting point. Do there exist any scarce resources which none the less are present in sufficient quantity for a part at least to be devoted not to sustaining human life, but to some other end? For any known human society the answer to this question is 'yes', for at least some of its members, and for some of the time. For any other species the answer (subject to some qualification in a few special cases) is 'no'. Resources are scarce whenever, taking into account the work necessary to make them available, they are limited in quantity, particularly in relation to the quantity which might be consumed if they were freely available. This contrasts them with free goods, such as the air we breathe, which are super-abundant for any community. Surplus represents scarce resources such as they exist in a margin between essential human needs and actual availability. At this stage it is misleading to contrast surplus with deficit, for by the present definition a human community has no deficit so long as it survives, however miserably, on its available resources. In theory an economic anthropology of progressive starvation could be constructed, but it would prove to be a somewhat specialized subject, with surprisingly little research material to support it. One might speculate, for example on whether the Maya tribes who built the vast temple complexes in the lowlands of Yucatan died out as a result of famine, but this helps little towards suggesting what the social consequences then might have been.[19] The fact is that all societies do have a surplus, and if some are held to be poor, this means only that their surplus is relatively small and precarious. This is not meant to exclude the possibility of some sudden catastrophe which destroys the surplus, and creates a real deficit in the same terms. In such case, by definition, the result can only be a reduction in population, which, undeniably, might have significant social consequences. The point must also be made that surplus, at every level, is an aggregate phenomenon. The young children in a family may of themselves have no surplus, but so long as they are nurtured by the older members, they share sufficiently in the aggregate surplus of the family.[20] This is a very elementary case, which need hardly be discussed further. But it can be extended to a much larger group, such as a whole tribe, which may well have much more elaborate means (of correspondingly greater interest to the anthropologist) of ensuring that a general surplus is distributed so that all needy individuals benefit from it. Here the simplest case arises where one primary staple crop is recognized in the local economy. Such is the finger millet grown by the Bemba of Zambia. The basic element in Bemba diet is a sort of porridge, called *Ubwali*, which is made out of millet.[21] It is eaten so long as the granaries still contain any grain from the last harvest. The three months in every year when the grain has run out are recognized as a period of hunger, with its own characteristic patterns of behaviour and social organization. This is a period of acute shortage, but not of chronic deficit, since the people expect to, and do, survive it. What is important is that there are prescribed obligations for sharing millet, which, because the society is matrineal, with men living with their wives, but away from the village of their own kin, involves constant provision for visiting relatives from other areas.[22] Tribute in grain is paid to the chiefs, wherever they travel in their domain, and is also sent to them in their own capitals.[23] There, they in turn must feed any hungry inhabitants.[24]

The Bemba provisions for distributing food do nothing to increase production, but this does not mean that they do not contribute to general welfare. At the same time any surplus is used for consumption, and never for investment for the future: in the nature of things this is out of the question. The whole economy, as is typical of any specialized agriculture, is at the mercy of the seasons and just as there are three hungry months, there are three months of relative abundance which follow the millet harvest. It is then, more than at any other time, that millet is used not only for *ubwali*, but for brewing a type of beer called *ubwalua*. Although this has important dietary values, it is an example of the use of surplus production. Significantly the brewing process is the most elaborate operation to take place in a normal household, but more important is the fact that it provides the common and essential way of fulfilling social obligations.[25] This is the point at which economy shades into tradition and culture, and fulfils an essentially non-economic role. It is also a good point for introducing the concept of involution.

The Bemba use of surplus millet to produce beer provides a relatively simple example of leisure, together with its social and political developments, according to the definition given on page 41. The important point is that at the end of every year the whole social, political and economic system, returns to its starting point, the whole round starts again. This is difficult to avoid for a simple agricultural people, whose whole pattern of consumption is inevitably geared to the annual round of the seasons. It provides an elementary example of involution, an essentially structural principle, which is found to apply whenever the use of the surplus resources of any social system, as laid down by tradition, is such as to ensure that the system always returns to the same point of equilibrium. It is the underlying principle of any homeostatic institution. A perfectly involuted social structure is governed by a rule of precedent (which is essentially cultural), which need never be modified, since its whole purpose is to ensure that in institutional terms, the social system to which it applies never evolves.[26] Involution is not necessarily confined to the economy of a society, but it commonly requires specialized economic institutions to support it. Involution is by no means static, although it is fundamentally opposed to innovation.

The dynamics of involution are well illustrated by the economic institutions of the Trobriand islanders, who live in a group of islands off the north coast of New Guinea. In contrast to the Bemba, who are shifting cultivators of cereals, the Trobrianders are fixed cultivators of root crops, particularly yams. Their villages are permanent, and are surrounded by gardens, there being one at least for each head of a household. Almost as important to him will be a ceremonial storehouse for yams, within the village itself, called a 'bwayma'.

The Trobrianders have a special word, 'malia', for the characteristic prosperity of their gardens.[27] This is turned to account by an elaborate scheme for sharing the garden produce among different individuals or groups connected with the owner. This is achieved, at the harvest season, by means of gifts made in the course of the special ceremonies called 'dodige bwayma'—filling the storehouse.[28] Here the most important contribution, which falls under a general heading of 'urigubu', comes from the kin of the owner's wife. This is comparable to the pattern of gifts among the Bemba, another matrilineal society. The total contributions received in a 'dodige bwayma' depends very much on rank and prestige, and a chief will receive vast tribute from many different groups.[29]

The yam-houses are beautifully decorated, and are important not only for establishing rank and precedence, but also for providing the yams consumed on important ceremonial occasions, such as the 'milamala'. This, the Trobriand new year, is the occasion when all the dead return to their village from their home on the island of Tuma, to be met by dancing and feasting.[30] Again, the death of any individual, is the occasion of vast distribution from the 'bwayma'.[31] There is also a special institution called 'buritila'ulo', when a quarrel between individuals from two separate villages is resolved by a competitive giving to each other of all their harvested resources. This is a legal institution with an economic base. This is but a special case: the super-abundance of yams also supports the political institution of chiefship, countless religious ceremonies, including the milamala, the whole social structure of kinship and the principles governing the allocation and use of land.

The involution which an economic system supports can operate within that system itself. A good example of this is provided by the wet-rice cultivators of Java. Their basic agriculture, which is shared by many other peoples in the same part of the world, raises a curious problem concerning its own origins, for it depends upon a type of original capital investment which proves so durable over the years and costs so much more to create, that there is little encouragement ever to repeat or extend it. The wet-rice paddy, known as 'sawah' in Java, is a flat, irrigated terrace, built by hand, at immense cost in labour, and carved out of a hill-side, where the natural drainage and precipitation provide the essential water supply. There is no danger of soil exhaustion or erosion, provided that the *sawah* complex is maintained year by year. Indeed some artificial systems of this kind have been in continuous use for more than 2000 years.[32] In any *sawah* the annual yield of rice can be varied between extraordinarily wide limits, according to how close together the seeds are planted, how many crops a year are sown, how carefully the irrigation is regulated or how much care is taken over weeding and transplanting. All these factors vary directly with the quantity of man-hours of labour supplied, so that wet-rice can almost always respond to a rising population through intensification, and so an ever increasing number of people can continue to live in an undepleted habitat. The involution in this case is demographic. The tendency is for surplus production always to be needed to support more people, and any tendency for social institutions to become more complex, indeed more involuted, because of population increases, is counteracted by relatively, but slowly, declining productivity per unit of labour. The farming operations themselves must become more complex, and therefore more time consuming: there is less time therefore to maintain, let alone develop, other institutions. The Javanese *sawah* farmers must run very hard to stay in the same place: in purely cultural terms they may even be moving backwards.[33]

In the examples so far given the economic base of involution has been provided by the agricultural staple of the relevant population— the millet of the Bemba, the yams of the Trobrianders, or the rice of the Javanese peasants. A more sophisticated case, and one with much greater possibilities of development, occurs when an involutionary system is maintained by the circulation of certain prescribed objects, which exist for no other purpose. A classic instance of this is the 'kula', an institution maintained among a group of islands in Melanesia, of which the Trobriands form one element.³⁴ *Kula* is the Trobriand word for ring, or circle, and the islands which take part in it, lie roughly in a circle in the part of the Pacific Ocean lying off the eastern end of New Guinea.

The islands are all quite distinct: the interesting point about *kula* is that it provides a common integrative factor in a complex of extremely diverse social and cultural institutions. In every different island *kula* is adapted to local institutions. But what is *kula*?

It consists primarily of a constant circulation of two different kinds of valuable ornament, known as '*soulava*' and '*mwali*'. The former are necklets made of small red shell discs, strung together; the latter are armlets made out of a single white sea-shell. Within *kula*, *soulava* only circulates clockwise, and *mwali* anti-clockwise. Only men participate, and in the Trobriands, only men of certain recognized villages and islands. Every participant has a number of special *kula* partners, ranging perhaps from two or three for a young man recently joined, to a hundred or more for an important chief. There must be at least one partner in each direction in the ring: this is so that one may receive *mwali*, and give *soulava* to, a partner in the clockwise direction, with a converse arrangment for an anti-clockwise partner.

The *mwali* and *soulava* are not all of the same value. The more important ornaments of each class have individual names, are famous throughout the *kula* ring, and confer immense prestige upon their possessor. Since, however, it is a rule of *kula* that the circulation of the valuables is constantly maintained, this prestige is inevitably somewhat temporary. It is still much sought after, and in practice the best-known ornaments are always traded from one chief to another.

The maintenance of *kula* requires a succession of overseas voyages, which are made in canoes specially built for the purpose. It is a rule that a voyage to another island is only to fetch *kula* valuables, never to bring them. So a Trobriander from the island of Kiriwina must sail to Kitava to bring home *mwali*, and to Dobu to bring home *soulava*. This means that Kitava must organize its own expedition to fetch *soulava* from Kiriwina, and Dobu do the same for *mwali*.

When a *kula* expedition arrives at its island destination, every member will seek out his own partners, and from them alone receive the appropriate *kula* objects. The voyages overseas involve such hazards, however, that they are organized only very occasionally, about once every two years in each direction, and all the *kula* participants sail together. *Kula*, therefore, adds up at one and the same time to both a communal and an individual venture.

Kula also subsists within each individual island, but without the elaborate ceremonial of an overseas expedition, and only as a private transaction between individual partners. Any particular *kula* valuable will be used alternately in overseas and inland transfers. For each of these two cases the social or political consequences will be quite different.

The extraordinary significance of *kula* can best be appreciated in the light of such abstract economic concepts as have already been applied in this chapter. *Kula* is clearly an almost perfect involutionary system according to the definition on page 49. It involves also an extremely elaborate use of leisure, according to a traditionally established corpus of precedent. This, though, is inherent in almost any homeostatic institution. *Kula* is much more original in its development of the idea of surplus for the additional production which it requires has nothing to do with the primary material subsistence of the people who participate in it. The *kula* valuables are useless for any purpose but that of *kula* itself, and in a derivative sort of way, of the institutions which depend upon it. In economic terms the *soulava* and *mwali* have no primary utility. They are not consumption goods (although the individual *kula* valuable does need to be replaced from time to time, thus supporting a minor enterprise among the fishermen of the Amphlett islands—between Kirwina and Dobu—who search the sea-bed for the necessary shells). Their meaning and use is entirely ritual, that is, prescribed by the local cultures, and extrinsic to their actual nature. The fact that they are clearly recognizable, relatively durable, and easily portable, makes them suitable, but never essential, for the purpose for which they are used. This inherent neutral quality of the *kula* valuables makes the institution which they support theoretically capable of indefinite extension and adaptation. True enough they are never used as a medium of exchange in trade (which would bring them close to what is normally understood as 'money'), but this limitation is purely a question of local tradition. The *kula* expeditions did provide the occasion for trade, as a sort of subsidiary activity, called *gimwali*, but this was seen as taking place on an entirely different level. A *kula* valuable would never be exchanged for trade goods.

One attribute, in particular, preserved the integrity of any particular *mwali* or *soulava*. This was the fact that it had its own recognized identity. A participant in *kula*, particularly an important one such as a chief, could well posses a fair number of *mwali* and *soulava* at any one time. But there would be no question of counting them so as to measure his total wealth, let alone in relation to that of any other participant. What the *kula* valuables bought was prestige, and this could well benefit more from the acquisition of a particular noted *soulava* or *mwali*, than from that of a large number of indifferent examples. This factor, perhaps more than any other, gave the whole institution of *kula* its unique character: it certainly inhibited its development and transformation into a purely commercial institution. It also allowed *kula* to subsist on the basis of purely natural products, that is the shells out of which the *mwali* and *soulava* were made. The master of the mint was the god of the ocean who made these shells: the fishermen of the Amphlett islands, who harvested them, have no significance apart from the fact that they happened to live over the natural sources of supply. Once, however, the value of a holding of *kula* valuables comes to depend merely on counting them up, then questions of authenticity become critical, and it is not long before uniform standards have to be maintained by some means of controlled production. If the *kula* valuables can be thought of as money, they were certainly never a coinage. Both, of their nature, are inherently products of involutionary systems, for otherwise they would have no purpose. Beyond this, however, coinage, both in its use and its political implications, has a significance never contemplated by the Melanesian islanders who brought their institution of *kula* to such astonishing refinement.

The most sophisticated theoretical treatment of *kula* is to be found in a supreme classic of economic anthropology, Mauss's 'The Gift'.[35] The constant theme of this work is that a gift always leaves behind an obligation to return the favour. It creates a sort of conventional indebtedness. The participant in *kula* who asks for a particular valuable from a partner who happens to have it, will always be given it, not because of some general principle of generosity, but because of the fact that the partner himself, because he also made such a request, and had it satisfied, took upon himself the obligation to meet any similar request made of him. The possession of any *kula* valuable, if it is the result of a *gift* (as it always will be) is always insecure, since it carries with it this obligation. And although it can never be given back to the giver (because of the prescribed direction for its circulation) the giver, being a *kula* partner, will always be able to command the gift of an appropriate *kula* valuable of the other kind. Once this principle of indebteness is recognized, convention alone is strong enough to enforce it, and no more is needed to maintain the whole involutionary system, or the network of subsisting relationships which it maintains.

But the theme of involution must be left, before it becomes overworked. A homogeneous self-contained economy, with no institutions for saving or investment, is not the only context for dealing with surplus, and there are other existing structures besides involution. But in social and historical terms involution is critical and always precedes the other possible structures. That is why it is so important. Its development and transformation will be a constant theme of the rest of this chapter.

LAND, ECONOMY AND SOCIETY

Land, in economic terms, is the most fundamental of all resources. All consumption goods, of whatever kind, are made out of raw materials which the land provides. Generally such provision is by means of organic processes, for which land is the essential substratum in ecological terms. Access to land, and to the right kind of land, and in sufficient measure, is therefore essential to any human population. The demand for land can be quite unspecific: land utilization by hunters and gatherers may well consist of nothing more than treating the whole of the available territory as a universal provider of all necessary resources, which, once reduced to possession —in the case of a plant by its being plucked or uprooted, or in the case of an animal by its being killed—become detached from the land, to be a part of the movable goods of the community occupying the territory. This is the essence of the nomadic way of life, and if land is superabundant in relation to the resource requirements of its inhabitants, then it may be seen as a free good in economic terms. This is an exceptional case: even a people such as the !Kung Bushmen recognize some demarcation of territory for economic and social ends, and endow some particular land-marks with a traditional role in their culture. Much more commonly land is the scarcest of all resources. Its scarcity (which is the best measure of its value) will depend on its use, and even more on the way in which any particular type of use is valued by its inhabitants. The use of land is always limited by such natural factors as climate, soil and topography, which determine, for example, the natural plant and animal species available for gathering and hunting, or at a more advanced level, the possible types of agriculture.

The use and exploitation of land provides the best possible model of the social and economic organization of the local population. The more diversified the local economy, the more advanced the technology applied in the production of essential resources, the higher the density of population, the more varied will be the types of land use, and, almost inevitably, the greater will be the complexity of all the different and conflicting interests which may subsist in the land. Taking again the case of the Chamulas, to whom all the above factors apply in very great measure, their land is seen to be divided into houseplots; *milpa* for the cultivation of the staple, maize; woodland to yield the wood needed as fuel, or for house construction; pasture, to graze the sheep whose wool is the basic raw material for all clothing; gardens and orchards for the vegetables and fruit which supplement the basic diet of maize; meadows which grow the thatch used for roofing, and finally the water-holes, to provide the most essential of all resources.

The division of Chamula territory into houseplots, *milpa*, woodland, pasture, gardens, orchards, meadows and water-holes, is largely, though by no means entirely, determined by natural features. The land, in its natural state, consisted almost entirely of woodland, with occasional above-ground sources of water, and the process of Chamula occupation has converted much of the woodland into other land-types, according to the needs of the local population. With such diversified land-use there was always a problem of maintaining equilibrium, which became the more acute, the greater the pressure of population. There must, for instance, be a certain balance between the area of woodland and the number of local inhabitants, for otherwise the need of the population for wood would exploit the available resources at a rate greater than that of natural replacement by means of new growth. In the earliest days of Chamula occupation trees were cleared, and wantonly burnt, merely so as to open up new land for *milpa*. Such wastefulness is much rarer at the present time, since population pressure has made Chamula aware of the need for conservation. None the less the need for wood in distilling, a booming local industry, with a substantial export market, may well be depleting the remaining forest resources at too high a rate.

Land scarcity tends to reduce to a question of the available area of the scarcest type of land. What this is, is determined by the characteristics of the local economy, which may well have to be adapted because of such scarcity. In Chamula there is a real deficit in *milpa*, in the sense that the population is quite unable to grow sufficient quantities of the staple maize. The adaptation, in this case, is to reliance on wage-earning opportunities outside the local territory, which means that the Chamulas are rapidly becoming a rural proletariat. This is a relatively advanced development in political and economic terms, and will be discussed in Chapter 5. The critical factor about the traditional Chamula local economy was that it was homogeneous, with the basic unit of production consisting of no more than the nuclear family, with an average of about four members. Every such small nucleated unit of this kind then had to have sufficient access to land of all the recognized types, which not surprisingly led to the development of an incredibly involved system of determining and allocating interests in land. Even today every Chamula family has its houseplot, an area of *milpa* (almost certainly inadequate) an interest in woodlands, a recognized source of thatch (if needed, for many houses now have tile roofs), and a right of access to a prescribed water-hole. All these interests are traditional, rather than commercial, in the sense that they are not acquired by purchase, but by some recognized method of prescription, or inheritance. The rules for allocation vary with the type of land, and for a dense population such as Chamula become very involved.

It is an inherent problem, of almost any culture, to assimilate land, which of its nature is integrated, durable and immovable, to the needs of the individual, who, in contrast, is isolated, mortal, and highly movable. The problem is resolved by a compromise. Any society will artificially sub-divide its land into different recognized interests, and according to different types of use. The main practical concern, as the case of Chamula illustrates, is with the produce of the land. At the same time as the land is sub-divided, the men whose lives it must sustain, are consolidated into different social groups, of which the typical Chamula nuclear family is but one example. This is a relatively short-lived group, and it is not surprising that Chamula house-sites, which represent the scarcest category of land, tend to be clustered into larger units, occupied by all the members of a patrilineal group, and their respective families.

The practice of establishing recognized corporations, corresponding to enduring interests in land, can go much further. The whole territory of Tiv is divided up according to a single principle, based on the recognition of individual *tars*, or patrilineally organized households, in such a way that a map of Tiv, showing the boundaries between different *tars*, provides at the same time a diagram of the social and political organization of the entire tribe—of approximately a million members.[36] This is a case of almost ideal harmony between descent and locality, time and space, as providing the basis of social structure. In other societies, such as the Nuer, with an economy dependent on seasonal transhumance, the principle of descent is dominant in deciding questions of land usage.[37] In others, such as those of the Javanese *sawah* cultivators, the principle of locality dominates the social structure.[38] The Nuer are preoccupied with the organization of the human community, which continues, in prescribed sub-divisions, wherever it may happen to be. The *sawah* cultivators are inevitably preoccupied with the organization of land resources, notably the paddy-fields, which are the stable, enduring and essential element in the life of the local community. The Tiv are a happy mean, somewhere between the two. In almost every case there is a close link between the allocation and use of land, and the structure of the local community. Understand one, and you can understand the other.

But there is more to land than this. It has a sort of mystical significance, which extends beyonds the range of any purely economic study. It is not only that certain landmarks, such as is the one single church in Chamula, which is regarded as the centre of the universe, and is the focus of the whole political and social life of the community, are key reference points in the local cosmology, but also that the land itself is the universal provider, and as such may be equated with women. There is a common cultural equation between them: land sustains society by production, women maintain society by reproduction. Rights over land and rights over women often go together, and may be thought of in similar terms: in each case the primary interest is in the yield.[39] This explains also the parallels which exist between religious rites relating to cultivation and those relating to sex. In each case the role of man is limited, and the completion of what man starts must be left to forces which can only be controlled by ritual means. This explains the elaborate garden and sexual image of the Trobrianders, which Malinowski needed nearly two whole books to describe.[40]

So also, the common mythopoeic origin of man is that he is fashioned out of the earth: this is how God made Adam. 'Dust thou art, and to dust thou shalt return.' Often, significantly, in primitive society there is a founding ancestress. Land is apt to enshrine the absolute cosmological principle: it embraces every dimension of human experience. It is the realm of the chief or king, who provides for all his people. It is sometimes, symbolically, his bride, This all explains why kingship is in part divine, as its associated rituals— particularly those associated with the death of the king—constantly declare. The great burial chamber of the Kabakas of Buganda is the holiest place in the whole country.[41] The idea of the consecration of land, however important in other parts of anthropology, particularly religion, points too far away from the economic themes of the present chapter, for it to be further considered here.

The important point is that land, considered as a resource, lies apart from other economic institutions, and is always treated according to different rules, for good social and cultural reasons. Even a people, such as the Chamula, with an almost modern economy, cannot deal with their own houses as they can with their sheep, or the maize in their granaries. Nor would they ever expect to be able to do so. Again, in the Anglo-American common law, or in any other legal system, land is treated as real or immovable property, a significantly different category from personal or movable category, in which all a man's other possessions lie. To some extent, therefore, this part of the present chapter is a digression, but it is an important one. It is however far too short and superficial. But if more were to be said, a different book would have to be writen, and it would be a book about land, and all its different facets. The subject is more than worthwhile: it just is not that of the present study.

DISTRIBUTION AND DIVERSIFICATION

The allocation of scarce resources, which is the constant preoccupation of economic theory, inevitably involves innumerable transfers of goods from producers to consumers. In human societies the underlying structures of production are never the same as those of consumption. The separation between the two may be greater for the more advanced societies, but even in those with the simplest social organization, there will be found an established pattern of resource distribution. The economic complexity of any social system can be measured according to the average population of the smallest absolutely self-contained economic unit. If this unit is seen as having defined boundaries, which will as likely be social as territorial, then there will be no movement of produce across them. In theory, at least, the members of such an economic unit could survive even if some disaster destroyed all other human kind.

This analysis must provide for the survival of all categories of people to be found in any given population. It must, for instance, provide for children without their being producers. There may be cases where the standard self-contained economic unit consists of no more than the nuclear family, but even for hunting and gathering populations dispersed over vast territories, such cases must be very rare. The whole concept, to be useful, must take into account the occasions when the greatest concentrations of population occur, say for an annual religious ceremony, or for a marriage between members of two different recognized groups. An example of this is the typical Nuer marriage inevitably between members of different lineages, where the woman's lineage will receive a prescribed number of cattle as bride-price.[42] This prevents any exogamous lineage from being a self-contained economic unit. Such institutions, such as those of religion and marriage described above, although primarily cultural or social, have the most significant economic consequences, particularly in making economic structures more complex and wide-ranging than they need to be for purely material reasons. Indeed, it is characteristic of a society such as the Nuer, that the recognized economic structure integrates a number of more or less identical units, judged by their patterns of production and consumption, which with a different underlying structure, could be entirely independent of each other. This is but one example of society creating, for social or cultural ends, economic institutions more complex, and more advanced, than are warranted by strictly economic factors.

In most cases the process of complexification goes so far as to make the smallest absolutely self-contained economic unit at least as large as the society in which it subsists. Indeed in a global society, that is, one which is absolutely self-contained in political and social terms, the two may be coincident. It is difficult to find a perfect example of this, but the Tikopia, as they were when they first became subject to anthropological study, were very close to being one.[43] But Tikopia is a small Pacific island, remote from any trade route, and so however interesting it may be, it is a somewhat special case.

The coincidence of social and economic systems is no accident. There is no more general human institution than that which expresses social relations in material terms: we need only look at the whole complex of the giving of presents in our own society. Such distribution of resources does not however require any corresponding diversification of production or consumption. A Nuer lineage receives cattle for the women it gives in marriage: it loses cattle for the women who marry into it. The fundamental economic transaction, which plays the most decisive role in extending and maintaining the socio-economic complex, particularly in societies with a simple economy, is indeed *gift*, and significantly what is given tends to be standardized. Such, for example, are the *kula* valuables of the Trobriand islands, but one can consider also how often in Europe and America flowers are given on social occasions (even to the point of including visits to the grave of a dead relative).

Diversification, in economic terms, can have two different meanings. The first is elementary. It is simply that within the economy more than one class of goods are produced and consumed. In this sense it would be difficult to find a human economy which was not diversified: even a people such as the Netsilik Eskimos who have only one basic resource, the seal, produce from it an astonishingly wide range of goods.[44] Economic diversification, in these terms, is a fundamental distinguishing feature of human kind. The second meaning of diversification presupposes asymmetric patterns of distribution within the total economy. In general terms this means that whatever group is considered within the economy, say from the nuclear family to the largest village, the exports of its own production are different in kind to the imports for its own consumption. In a diversified economy distribution serves ends which are economic, as well as social. It is tempting to characterize the modern state as being one in which the ends of distribution are exclusively economic, but this overstates the true position.

The idea of diversification provides the means of making a fundamental distinction, originally formulated by Emile Durkheim, between two different kinds of social structure. In the first identical small-scale diversified economic units repeat themselves across the whole fabric of the local society, so that in the aggregate they constitute the whole of its corporate economic structure. If two such units combine, the result is no more than another unit of similar structure, but larger in scale. The basic diversified unit may well be no more than the nuclear family. Thus in the traditional society of Chamula, the father, as head of the family, was responsible for cultivating the *milpa*, and so providing the family with maize, its basic food resource, while the mother (helped by the children, where possible) looked after the sheep, whose wool provided the basic resource needed for clothing. There were of course other tasks to be fulfilled, such as fetching wood and making tortillas, but these too were allocated to specific members of the family, thus maintaining the essential structure of its diversified economy. The total economy of Chamula *was* merely the sum of these separate family economies, integrated by prescribed canons of distribution, or better perhaps, redistribution. Using Durkheim's term, a society with such an economy has *mechanical* solidarity.[45] The economy itself will inevitably be a subsistence economy, in the sense that every unit within it produces goods of precisely the same type as its itself consumes. (The fact of distribution means that it does not always consume its own actual produce.) This structure can be preserved even in the case of two or more complementary economies existing side by side, provided that they are discreet social systems, each with its own mechanical solidarity. This is a fairly common model of socio-economic symbiosis. Thus, for example, some of the Trobriander islanders are fishermen, rather than cultivators, but the two classes exchange their produce. In this case the two economies have the same underlying social structure, but this need not be so. In the interlacustrine states of East Africa, the same territory is often the home of a dominant minority of pastoralists and a subservient majority of cultivators, each with its own social and cultural institutions, but with prescribed exchanges between the two.[46] In West Africa the highly nomadic Fulani lead their herds of cattle across the territory of a wide variety of sedentary cultivators, with a suitable symbiotic relationship prescribed with each separate group.[47] In all these cases each discrete class largely preserves its own subsistence economy: the products of the other classes are essentially marginal.

The division of a society into different classes, each defined according to a particular economic specialization, with a traditional symbiosis between them all, can develop to an astonishingly high level of complexity. The classic example of this is the Hindu caste system, in which every caste—or indeed sub-caste—defines a particular endogamous social category, each one of which has, at least in theory, an *undifferentiated* economy. There quickly comes a point along this line of development when some groups, at least in terms of their nominal economic classification, no longer constitute a self-contained subsistence economy. Plainly barbers in India, who constitute a well-defined sub-caste, are not as such anywhere near to having a subsistence economy of their own. This does not matter, for two reasons: the first is that caste-occupation almost invariably combines with a basic subsistence occupation, such as agriculture; the second is that the prescribed redistribution of produce within the caste system ensures that each specialized occupation receives a sufficient share of essential resources.[48]

The caste system is perhaps the greatest known elaboration of the principle of mechanical solidarity, but in the relationship between the different castes Durkheim's second kind of social structure, that of organic solidarity,[49] becomes apparent. The essential concept here is that it is not necessary for an individual, a family or any larger group to have any direct command over the resources essential to it, provided that it is an integral part of a socio-economic system which has reliable institutionalized means of making these resources available to it. For example, a family—such as the typical urban family in Europe or America—need not produce a single essential foodstuff, provided that it has some prescribed access to food resources sufficient for its own needs. It is easy to take access for granted, as well as such supporting institutions as the money to buy food with, and the stores to buy it in, but they are by no means essential, and represent an extremely late and specialized stage in the development of human economy. Organic solidarity can well exist at a much less advanced stage of institutional development. Many societies are in a transitional stage between the two: a typical case is the peasant community, such as Chamula, partially dependent upon a local market town.

At the most elementary level of a differentiated economy, it is sufficient that every unit in the economy should be able to contribute the surplus of its own production to the total economy of which it is a part, in exchange for a share, to be consumed by itself, of the aggregate surplus production of the rest of the economy. In a pure exchange economy no single unit, according to the established consumption patterns, produces a subsistence staple. Such are the economies of Europe and North America, but they are so complex, particularly in relation to the political institutions which support them, that they are an unsatisfactory starting point for considering the characteristic institutions of organic solidarity. It is better to start with a purely theoretical case, to see the problems which it raises, and the sort of institutions which it generates, and then to apply the results to specific societies studied by anthropologists.

The theoretical model proposed is of a total economy divided into a number, say N, of equal units, according to population, with each unit producing the entire population's consumption needs of one essential resource. The different units may be regarded as occupying different, though adjacent, territories, each one having physical characteristics favourable to the production of its particular resource. Then all that need be done is for every unit to divide its production into N equal parts, keep one for itself, and of the remainder to consign one to each of the other N-1 units. It is to be noted that nothing is being said about exchange, at least any form of contractual exchange, let alone any mention of sale or the use of money. The only trouble with this model is that it is totally unrealistic, particularly in relation to basic human consumption needs. It can be modified by allowing the N different units to be unequal, the size of each one being proportional to the overall demand for its product. This still requires an economic stability, supported by fixed relative population trends in the different units, which could hardly occur in practice. To some extent the Hindu caste system is a solution to the problem in these terms, but its consequences are extraordinarily involved, and have to be supported by a number of institutional expedients of a political character, which in pure economic terms are almost certainly counter-productive.

The model itself is wasteful in terms of human energy. If the territory of the total population is at all extensive, then the distribution of goods required by the system will demand a good deal of time, which might otherwise be devoted to increased production. It is clear, then, that the distributive sector of such an economy must develop extremely efficient institutions, if it is to justify itself in purely economic terms. At the same time some increase in productive efficiency is desirable even for the support of the most efficient distributive system; this is not so important a factor as might appear at first sight, since, as any number of existing field studies make clear, a quite *un*differentiated economy, such as that of the Bemba,[50] for example, can still support a wide-ranging distributive system.

Two particular institutions, each of considerable antiquity, developed independently in many different areas to furnish local economies with an efficient system of distribution and exchange. The first of these is the market: the idea of the market is simply for there to be a time and place established by tradition as a focus for the distribution of produce. The time should regularly recur, say once every five days, and the place should be equally accessible for all users of the market. If then, for a differentiated economy, there was one market centre, with a market every five days, and within a day's return travel for every user, then the market would be efficient in economic terms for the model proposed above, so long as one day in five of lost production was more than compensated for by the advantage of every producer being able to consume an equal share of the produce of all the others. This, in fact, is a measure of the incentive which the market offers to any potential user of it.

Incentive is a critical factor in the operation of any economy: it is what determines one course of action, against another (including, possibly, inaction). So with the introduction of the market one can postulate that it provides sufficient incentive for every producer to distribute outside his own sphere of production a prescribed fraction of his produce. This allows the original model to be made somewhat more realistic: every economic unit divides its production into two parts, one to be retained, the other to be distributed through the market. The latter part is then divided into N-1 shares, one for each of the other economic units. Once this is done, it makes no difference to the working of the model, if the retained production is in every case of the same resource. This is the case with the Tiv of Nigeria, who have a very comprehensive market network, but who are, at the same time subsistence cultivators of millet.[51] This does not of itself exclude millet from the market, which indeed can provide the mechanism for reallocating the staple from those with a surplus to those with a deficit.

If, however, the staple crop is largely outside the market, what then are the N essential resources, differentially produced within the total economy, which the original model requires? The question becomes clearer if 'essential' is defined entirely according to what the local culture deems to be indispensable or at least highly desirable, throughout the whole economy. Such is the distilled alcohol produced in a number of Chamula villages. Typical market goods are craft products, or fruit and vegetables, coming from only one sector of the local economy. This, then ties up with traditional local skills, or particular areas uniquely favourable to certain types of intensive cultivation. Here again, Chamula provides a good example, with one village producing hats, another musical instruments, a third apples, and so on.

The second institution which developed to provide a more efficient system of distribution, is trade.[52] If trade is no more than the exchange of goods inherent in the whole distribution process of a differential economy, then it is a tautology. But trade can be, and often is, an institution in its own right. Here it is best understood in connection with the specialized role of the trader, that is, a person who provides a living for himself, and his household, by participating in the distribution process, without being either the producer or consumer of the goods which he handles.

How then does the trader make his living? Or putting the question another way, what incentive does he offer to others, whether consumers or producers, to deal with him? Let us return to the original model on page 62. Suppose that one of the N essential resources consists simply of the services offered by the trading sector of the economy. The reward of this sector will then consist of a share, equal to the proportion of traders in the total economy, of all the other resources. If all sectors are of equal size, then the traders will get an N-th part of all these resources. What, then, does the trader offer in exchange? Quite simply the answer is contact between original producers and ultimate consumers. Taking the case of the market which occurs every five days (and noting that traders can operate without there being any markets at all), then, without the trader, every producer in fact engages in two activities, production and exchange. The trader allows the producer to stick to production. The incentive, if in somewhat simple terms, is that the producer, by not having to go to market every fifth day, can increase his production by a quarter. If the trader is content with less than this, then the producer will gain by dealing with him. The trader is the middle-man, sometimes despised because he can get more for his services, than his clients can get from him for their products, but this means only that in terms of the goods produced for exchange, the services he offers are more valuable to any sector of the economy than his rateable share of its total produce. In competitive economic terms, and in a perfect market, the answer would be for men to be tempted away from production into distribution, and this does happen, time and time again.

What is significant about trade is that it can extend the chain linking original producer with ultimate consumer to almost any length, simply by adding more trading links to it. This will be possible so long as the ultimate consumers, in real terms, will be ready to stand the cost of the share of what they consume which must go to every trader in the chain. So long as the demand continues to exist with every additional link in the chain, there will be sufficient incentive for some particular man to forge a new link. This process explains how a natural product such as, say, the avocado pear, can be an item of popular daily consumption in one area, such as the Mexican state of Chiapas, and a comparatively rare luxury in another, such as New York City. Quite simply, for every avocado pear which reaches New York City, a dozen people along the line have consumed one—or, if not actually consumed it, traded it off to get their own livelihood.

Trading and markets are essentially independent: traders can link two markets together, but equally they can by-pass markets altogether. What is important is that together they constitute the distributive sector of any economy: this is critical, since this sector is the one capable of the greatest development, elaboration, extension, and in institutional terms, innovation. The yardstick is always efficiency, perhaps the most important factor for growth in economic history. For the anthropologist the important factor is the new social and political institutions which an increasingly efficient distributive economy generates. These are considered in Chapter 5. For the present analysis it is the differentiation of products and services which makes distribution economically significant. And once the idea catches on, it has a snowball effect. Economic diversification is not only a product of an increase in the size of the total economy, it also encourages such increase, almost exponentially, This explains how the world, almost within the last hundred years, has become a total economy. Production may have become more efficient, but this is nowhere so important as the increased efficiency of the distributive sector. Poor distribution can completely nullify efficient production, where good distribution can often overcome the defects of inefficient production. The small-scale Indian coffee-growers in the remote Southern Mexican township of Pantelhó,[53] whose produce is consumed on the world's breakfast tables, provide but one example of this. Their rewards may be small, particularly in relation to the price which the ultimate consumer pays for their product, but the production itself is still economic. This is a critical factor in development studies, and makes almost a special—and very important—case, out of the social anthropology of the distributive economies of the third world. Something will be said of this in Chapter 9, but the whole subject really deserves a study of its own.

MONEY AND MONETARY INSTITUTIONS

The distribution of products in a diversified economy, at least when it takes place through markets and trade, almost inevitably comes to depend upon the institution of exchange. The typical market or trade transaction consists of two people who accept each other's goods at a prescribed rate of equivalence, for example, one hat against a basket of apples. A diversified economy can subsist without such exchange transactions: there could, for instance, be a traditional obligation, resting upon all producers, to distribute their output in prescribed shares or quantities among all other producers, as in the Hindu caste system.

Once, however, exchange of goods becomes the normal means of distribution, then for each new category of goods which is introduced into the sphere of exchange, the number of new exchanges which become possible is equal to the number of already existing categories. In mathematical terms, with n categories exchanged, there are $\frac{1}{2}n(n-1)$ possible exchange transactions, with the same number of possible rates of exchange, needless to say. In a perfect system of exchange every producer expects to be able to exchange his own products for prescribed quantities of another's products, with no possible fluctuations in the rates of exchange. For an economy with more than a mere handful of different products such a system of exchange would be quite impossible to maintain. It would require not only a constant rate of production of all goods exchanged, but an equally constant demand for them at the prescribed rates of exchange. The problem becomes the more difficult when it is seen that the production of many of the goods is inevitably seasonal, and then can vary from year to year, both in quantity and quality. Plainly some institutional means is necessary to simplify the whole system of exchange.

One solution would be to have a number of special operators in the market, who would carry sufficiently large stocks of all goods exchanged, so that they could always accept any exchange offered to them. Their contribution to the economy would consist not of goods, but of these exchange services, which would provide a living for them by means of some sort of commission or margin. This is a stable workable system so long as it rests upon other stable factors relating to production, demand and so on. Indeed it is potentially extremely flexible, for so long as all exchanges are carried out by one recognized sector of the economy, there will be a relatively efficient mechanism for varying the rates of exchange, so as to equate the demand for any product with the supply available. It is a curious fact, however, that although the present analysis is concerned with the simplest possible diversified economies (and nothing has been said about he use of money in exchange), the best actual example of a specialized pure exchange sector of an economy is to be found in the open foreign exchange markets in money which flourish in a number of countries. In Jerusalem, before the six-day war of 1967, there were any number of small foreign-exchange dealers ready to exchange any major currency for any other, at prescribed rates.[54]

Why, in fact, was the Jerusalem foreign-exchange market so successful, and what lessons can be drawn from this success so as to construct a model reasonably applicable to simple economies. The first point is that the Jerusalem market dealt in an inherently limited number of different categories of goods: the number of world currencies is somewhere around 150, but the number available in the Jerusalem market was probably around ten—the Dollar, the Pound, the French and Swiss Francs, the D-Mark, the Guilder, the Lira, and so on, so as to include all the world's major currencies, with each having constant undifferentiated quality. Secondly, one dollar is by definition as good as any other dollar, and five dollars is always worth exactly five times one dollar. The third point is that the utility of the goods exchanged is so generalized and intensive in economic terms as to be almost immune from any but the largest scale upheavals. The fourth point is that the goods exchanged have almost indefinite durability, particularly in view of the fact that the actual physical condition of any one of them has no effect on its value: an old worn bank-note can always be exchanged for a brand-new one of the same denomination. The fifth point is that the demand for the goods exchanged is extremely high in relation to their bulk: just consider the bulk of the goods which can be got in exchange for a handful of bank-notes in a supermarket.

Returning now to the case of a specialized exchange sector in a differentiated economy, one can consider it in the light of these five points. As to the first, relating to the number of categories of goods, this in practice is astonishingly high for any human population, let alone one with so sophisticated an institution as a specialized exchange sector of its economy. Many an anthropologist has tried to count the different types of goods displayed in a remote and isolated market, only to find that fifty or sixty is a relatively small total. As to the second point, the quality of the goods is far from constant: indeed a major part of the problem is that many categories only come into the market in a particular harvest season. Turning to the third point, utility tends to be highly specialized: a hat can only be worn on the head. A possible exception to this is the agricultural staple, where such exists, for by definition it meets the universal and generalized needs of the total population for food-stuffs. The fourth point does apply in some cases, notably for any craft goods, such as pottery, which do tend to be relatively durable, even though they are subject to wear and breakage. It applies to agricultural produce only to a limited degree. Fifth, and last, all goods in a simple economy tend to be bulky: this factor, as much as any other, restricts the size of such economies.

Apparently, then, a specialized exchange sector by itself provides no more than a very partial solution to the distribution problems of a differentiated economy. Suppose, however, that within the exchange sector one (or possibly more) categories of goods are carried simply because they have a constant undifferentiated quality (point two), a completely generalized utility in exchange (point three), indefinite durability (point four) and extremely small bulk—and therefore high portability (point five). What advantages would then follow? First, because nothing would ever be lost by accepting this new category, which may be defined as 'money', it would be universally acceptable. Even in such a case as that where a hatter found a market-gardener ready to exchange a basket of apples for one of his hats, nothing would be lost by having two transactions, the first exchanging the hat for money, and the second exchanging the money back into the basket of apples. But now, because nothing is lost by having two transactions, there is no problem in separating them, whether in space or time, so that the hatter can get his apples from a different man to the man who got the hat from him, and at a different time. This can go a long way to solving problems of a producer with a seasonal market. If confined to immediate exchange for other produce, he has a real problem in supporting his household out of the market season: but with money, he needs only to save for this time, and his problem is solved.

Money, at this elementary level, has two main attributes: it is a universal medium of exchange, and it is an indefinite store of the power to effect an exchange. Money, in this sense, is an abstract concept, but for it actually to be used it must be given unique concrete expression in some recognized category of goods, having the properties of uniformity, durability and portability. Such goods are called 'specie', and their production and distribution raise a number of rather intractable problems, particularly in relation to the origin of money in any economy.

What resources and skills must exist in a pre-monetary economy for it to be able to produce uniform, durable and portable specie?

This question is by no means so elementary as it must seem at first sight in a culture which takes the existence of specie absolutely for granted. A people such as the Nuer have no means of combining the resources and skills available to them so as to produce anything with the required specifications. It is significant that their cattle, which are uniform as to species, relatively durable (being even the more so if their ability to reproduce themselves is taken into consideration) and portable in the sense that they may be herded more or less at the will of their owner, are used as a sort of specie, although in a very restricted sphere of exchange. The Trobriand islanders, with their *kula* valuables, have something which comes closer to specie, and which could become a specie if the idiosyncrasies of each particular example were to be disregarded. The fact that the *kula* valuables exist in two kinds is not a fatal objection, although if they were to become monetized, the kind which was easier to produce would almost certainly drive the other out of circulation.[55] Salt is sometimes a product of elementary technology, which at the same time can be used as specie.[56] There are indeed countless examples of so-called primitive moneys: in every case there must be broad limits to the amount of specie available. For it must never become so abundant that it is easier to acquire from its original source, than it is by means of exchange, for then no-one would ever exchange anything for it, and its essential use as a medium of exchange would be eliminated. Such, however, is the utility of money, in pure economic terms, that if the supply is increased the natural reaction is never to demonetize, but always to devalue the specie in terms of the goods for which it is exchanged. So also, specie has to become in very short supply before it ceases to be useful, for goods can then always be devalued in terms of it. Nor is the revalution of specie essential to deal with variations in the quantity circulation in relation to the exchange transactions for which it is required, since the velocity of circulation, that is the number of transactions per unit of specie, can also be varied between very wide limits. None the less there are two critical thresholds for the quantity of specie: above the higher threshold specie becomes so abundant that everyone loses confidence in it;[57] below the lower threshold the supply becomes so short that everyone tends to hoard, and the specie goes out of circulation, and is no longer used in exchange transactions.

With a stable population, and a stable economy, specie must be produced in just such amounts as will replace the amounts lost, but the question then is, who is to be the producer? Plainly production must be subject to some centralized control, which suggests a monopoly, and this is a very common case. But as always about money, there is something of a paradox, in that a society of the necessary sophistication to establish and protect an economic monopoly, for whatever purpose, is likely already to be monetized. It is natural enough that where such a monopoly does exist, then it will be the prerogative of the central government of the people concerned, if such exists. It is not for nothing that the head of the sovereign has always appeared on British coins.

The problem is bypassed if the specie used within the community comes from outside it. Any community, given a certain amount of such exogenous specie in circulation, can always maintain the supply simply by exporting enough produce in every year to whatever other community it is that the specie originates in. One may well have a number of independent communities such that the whole export economy of one of them depends upon the export in specie in just this way. An example of this is the Balaya of New Guinea who manufacture standardized salt-blocks for use as specie by all their neighbours.[56]

Specie should not be thought of as the only kind of money. Theoretically, at least, it could be altogether eliminated. Suppose for instance, that in England or the United States everyone was required to hold a bank-account, and all monetary transactions had to be by cheque, what use would there then be for specie? Why, indeed, does specie survive at all? The answer is that simply as money it carries more confidence among the people who use it than anything else. The transactional use of money is a ritual, in that the whole meaning of the money is extrinsic to its physical characteristics.[58] If you take a coin out of your pocket, and look at it, there is nothing inherent in its nature which shows how it can be used, or indeed that it has any use. Indeed, if you melt the coin down it will be nothing more than the metal contained in it, which may be worth no more than a fraction of its nominal value as a coin. Again the coin may be obsolete, like an old English penny, which lost all its value when the British government, which made it in the first place, declared that it no longer had confidence in it. The pre-eminent confidence in specie does not mean however that other types of money are altogether excluded.

The whole question of lending money at interest, and the creation of debts for money so lent, which can themselves be used as money, is too complex for the present study. But the fact that money is a store of the power to effect transactions does provide a strong incentive for those who hold money, but have no immediate transactions for which they wish to use it, to make it available, on terms profitable to themselves, to others who do have such transactions, but have no money. The idea that money can be sold in terms of itself is much more sophisticated than the idea of money itself, and like many similar institutions, was considered immoral or unclean when it first appeared. The price paid for money in these terms is called interest, and the selling of money in this way was originally called usury, which in the Christian Europe of the early Middle Ages was a purely Jewish institution, since no Christian could engage in it without mortal sin.[59]

Usury is in fact the whole basis of modern banking, which provides a purely monetary facility by means of having every transaction or repayment effected by debiting one account, and crediting another with the like amount. In such a case no specie changes hands, and nothing need exist which has any value in monetary terms. Plainly the sum of all accounts, both those in credit and those in debit, and including that of the bank itself, is zero at any one time. The pay-off for the bank lies in the fact that it charges interest on the accounts in debit, and if it pays any on those in credit it is at a lower rate.

Theoretically the banking facility is highly inflationary. So long as a bank honours the transactions of its clients, it can effectively put any amount of new money in circulation. There are a number of disincentives which operate. First, every bit of new money which a bank creates means extending the credit of one of its clients, and the bank itself may become concerned about just how credit-worthy its clients may be. (It is agreed by all monetary theorists that any advanced economy would be reduced to absolute chaos if the banks called in all overdrafts: there is thus a sort of illusion, requiring a considerable act of faith, underlying the whole idea of the bank.) But this anxiety on the part of banks is not enough, and it is no accident that the banking sector of any economy is subject to considerable state control. The classic form of this is to require the banks to grant a considerable part of their credit to the state, in exchange for assets such as specie whose value the state itself guarantees. Even this may not be enough, and the state may further restrict the granting of credit by banks, often in a quite arbitrary way.[60]

All this may be far removed from the simple societies studied by the anthropologist, but the underlying ideas, such as that of debt, are understood even in such societies. And the idea that debts may be treated as money is not too difficult for a people such as the Chamulas, or their neighbours, the Zinacantecos, to grasp. It has, for one thing, the great advantage of compensating for the shortage of specie, and this is critical for the Chamulas, since their specie, which is no more than the Mexican Peso, comes from outside. It is amazing to see how independent the Chamula economy has become as a result of monetary institutions, of the nature of banking, generated within itself.

Money is the second most important original creation of human kind. The first is language, which is considered in Chapter 7. Money is different from language, in that while no human society is without language, many are recorded as being without money. Language is the hall-mark of man since his earliest beginnings; money quickly followed the emancipation of man from his hunting and gathering economy—although strictly there is no reason why hunters and gatherers should not have money. Money, too, is connected with language, since it requires the ability to count, that is to create words for numbers to an indefinitely high level, and not all languages are capable of this. Those that are require principles for the organization of vocabulary, which, linguistically, are quite unique. Indeed, where the money used inside a linguistic community originates outside it, the numbers used in counting money tend to be adopted from the same external source.

The development of banking, and the extension of the idea of money which goes with it, parallels the linguistic development of literacy.[61] It is significant that the earliest known written texts often record monetary matters. Money is the most original and most successful of all economic institutions. It corresponds to the reality that distribution is the key to any human economy: it can provide the model of any distributive system. The underlying structure of any society which uses money is well represented by the pattern for the circulation of money. And yet money itself is no more than what is agreed to be money: tradition established the meaning of money, just as it establishes the meaning of language. But money is more pervasive than language: one can learn to use a foreign money much more easily than a foreign language. The institutions of money are more adaptable, more universal, and yet language comes first. A child learns to talk, before it learns to count. The answer is that the political and economic presuppositions of money are not universal: indeed, historically, they are extraordinarily recent. Yet money is so powerful that one can make the historical generalization that in any kind of competition between two peoples, the one which has the superior monetary institutions will win over the other. Money is the factor which has made powerful peoples with relatively scarce natural resources: it is no accident that Italy in the fourteenth, or Flanders in the fifteenth, or England in the seventeenth century achieved an economic pre-eminence hardly to be explained in terms of their natural resources.

Money as a cultural institution has been little studied by anthropologists. This contrasts with the enormous preoccupation with money of contemporary economists. Their limitation is that they take for granted institutions which may well not exist in the societies studied by anthropology. The true meaning of money remains obscure to scholars from either side.

5

Economy and Society

The importance of economics to the anthropologist lies in the fact that the complex of economic institutions in any society determines, more than any other factor, its whole political and social organization. Chapter 4 surveys the different human institutions which can combine with natural resources so as to constitute the economy of any particular society. The underlying principle is always one of organization: even at the most elementary level man's use of resources depends upon a cycle of production, consumption and distribution, which requires conscious organization on his part. This requirement makes even the simplest human society extraordinarily complex in comparison to that of any non-human population. The simple societies, which are the subject of the present section, are essentially homeostatic,[1] so that the principles on which they are organized are purely traditional, and are transmitted from one generation to another simply by a process of education. This presupposes that the essential natural resources are constantly available, with seasonal variation it may be, in sufficient quantity to maintain the local population. The reason why production requires organization is that no human population lives in an environment with natural resources sufficient for its needs, which can be exploited without the application of labour. This may be defined as the directed use of human energy to economic ends, primarily of production, particularly in the case of simple small-scale societies. Economic efficiency measures output, in these terms, in relation to the input of labour. At this elementary level, labour is the most important factor in production. An important reason why simple societies are organized according to the principle of mechanical solidarity is that labour does not need to be very highly differentiated in order to produce needed consumption goods, while at the same time the volume of production is directly proportional to the input of labour. The relative complexity of consumption demands, combined with the different labour potentials within every family, inevitably leads to the requisite labour being divided into different categories, each with its own specialized economic purpose, and each being allocated to different social categories. Thus it is that every member of a nuclear family has his own recognized tasks, like the father in the Chamula family who works the *milpa* for maize, and fetches wood, and the mother who herds the sheep (often helped by her older children), and cooks the tortillas.

The economic requirements of a simple society may be such that the nuclear family is too small a unit, so that larger units must be organized for the purposes of essential economic co-operation.[2] So long, however, as the local economy remains simple enough, there will be a maximal unit, which in purely economic terms could exist independently of the rest of the local economy. This maximal unit must be constituted in social terms, that is by defining rules of membership, largely in terms of one sort of relationship existing between the members, and another with non-members. These rules are an essential part of the underlying social structure of the society. This explains why rules based upon kinship, such as are explained on page 29, are so widely adopted: the principle of defining membership is already established in biological terms.

Once the maximal economic unit is defined for a simple society, then as already explained on page 59, the total society is no more than the aggregate of these separate units. The integration of these units by economic means, notably distribution, has a political, and not an economic rationale. In economic terms it is inefficient, and can only be maintained by a traditional use of surplus production, or perhaps better, of surplus labour. It is characteristic of marginal economies, where a small population subsists precariously on the resources of an extensive territory, that in seasons with no surplus production, the local society fragments into its separate maximal units, with little contact taking place between them. Durkheim elaborated this theme to the point of associating the highest level of religious activity of any population with the occasions of its greatest concentration in one place.[3] In economic terms such activity is a wasteful use of labour and resources, most likely to occur in times of the greatest surplus, so Durkheim's theme has a clear economic basis. It is, as almost any generalization, an over-simplification, and later scholars have produced a number of counter-examples.[4]

The size of the maximal unit in any economy is largely determined by the extent of the local division of labour. Labour decides the economic role of any individual, but plainly anyone with more than one task assigned to him, will have more than one such role. Thus the head of the Chamula family has the roles of cultivator, wood-gatherer and so on. He has not so much one role, as a particular role-set. The best measure of the division of labour is the number of different *economic* role-sets.[5] In a society with mechanical solidarity, this number will largely determine the size of the maximal unit, but it does not have to be very large before the economy becomes too complex to be that of a society with such an elementary structure. Indeed organic solidarity characterizes any society in which the maximal economic unit has become co-extensive with whole population: this is the case with any modern economy.

At first sight a simple society appears to be one in which all role-sets are essentially productive in economic terms. Every maximal unit is a co-operative producing for its own consumption. This analysis immediately disregards the inherently unproductive members of any society, for instance, such of its children as are too young to participate in the economic process. It is not sufficient to dismiss them as marginal consumers: in some cases tradition makes them privileged consumers, as witness the care given to Bemba children during the lean months of the year.[6] It is far better to accept that some role-sets are negative in economic terms, that is, those who hold them are parasitical on the economy as a whole. Such role-sets are counterbalanced by those which are positive, so that if a numerical index could be given to every role-set, there would be a zero-sum over all.

The concept of parasitism is extremely useful in the development of a political economy. It corresponds to the fact that any economy has a surplus. It is tolerated for children, needless to say, because they will themselves grow up to be positive factors in the local economy. Children represent the most important investment for the future in any simple society. But children are by no means the only case of parasitism: any number of other role-sets exist which are equally parasitical. In the simple mechanical society they can stand apart from the generalized social structure.[7] A common example is that of the holy man, supported by society because the ritual which he alone can perform is thought to be beneficial, whether it is to bring favourable weather, or to cure sickness, or whatever. Another people may have a chief or king, supported by tribute of its economic staple, who is the focus of political organization. In economic terms these roles stand outside the sector of primary production, but it is mistaken to assume that they make no economic contribution. After all the holy man who brings the right weather and preserves good health certainly contributes to the efficiency of the local production: so also, a king may stand at the head of a political organization which can be so well mobilized for defence, that his subjects can live in peace, without fear of attack from neighbouring peoples.[8] This can only enhance the local economy.

In any study of the division of labour, the chiefs and the holy men must not be left out of account. Rather should one consider how precisely to characterize their contribution in economic terms. What they offer is best called 'utility', an imponderable contribution, inherent in their roles, which enables the rest of the economy to be carried on more efficiently. One may go further than this, and divide society into two economic classes, the first offering 'produce', the second, 'utility'. This is a rough and ready division, but it is useful for further analysis. For if the economically active population be N, divided in the ratio of p to u (with $p+u=1$) between the suppliers of *produce* and *utility*, with a total productivity P for any given value of p, then the contribution of *utility* (U) will increase productivity, P, so long as $P>P_1$, P_1 being the value of P when $p=1$, and $u=0$, which is the case when there is no sector of the economy which contributes *utility*. The critical factor is the contribution of utility to every unit of production. Now for P_1, the productivity of each of the N members of the active working population is quite simply $\frac{P_1}{N}$. But for P $(>P_1)$, only pN persons are productive, so the unit productivity becomes $\frac{P}{pN}$. If therefore, $P>P_1$, then, dividing both sides by pN,

$$\frac{P}{pN} > \frac{P_1}{pN} = \frac{p+u}{pN} P_1, \text{ (since } p+u=1).$$

$$= \left(1 + \frac{u}{p}\right) \frac{P_1}{N}.$$

This inequality means that for a sector uN, of the total population N, to add to the efficiency of the local economy, its contribution of utility to the producers (pN in number) must be such as to increase their average productivity by an amount, $\frac{u}{p}$, that it is the ratio of the utility sector's population to that of the productive sector. If, for example $u = \dfrac{1}{3}$, and $p = \dfrac{2}{3}$, the unit productivity of the producers must be increased by a half. This analysis can be made more sophisticated, but it is sufficient for the present stage.

If one takes the simplest societies, where u represents the kings and holy men, it will be a small proportion, in conventional mathematical terms, $\mathcal{E}$, of the total population. In this case it need only increase unit production by $\mathcal{E} \dfrac{P_1}{N}$ to justify itself. In fact we know that the holy men do not bring rain or cure sickness, or even that the enemies against whom the king offers protection would never attack in any event, so that however small $\mathcal{E}$ may be, it does nothing to increase unit productivity, not even by an amount equal to itself. Our superior knowledge in fact counts for nothing: it is not what we know, but what the actual population think they know, which counts, and after all they only need a surplus greater than $\mathcal{E} \dfrac{P_1}{N}$ per unit of production, for them not to realize that their kings and holy men are essentially counter-productive. This condition can be satisfied by even the poorest economies.

Suppose, however, the $\dfrac{P_1}{N}$ represents a really positive sector of the economy, providing essential craft skills, say in the fields of pottery or textiles, it then could well increase productivity by a far greater factor than it itself represented, viewed as a fraction of the total population. Then the whole analysis, based upon the simple society, becomes unstable. Up to a certain point the relatively small maximal unit can continue to exist, either by having every craft represented within it, by a prescribed minority, or by having it exercised, as a sort of by-line, by every producer. The latter solution is only possible where the necessary skills are not too specialized. The former solution runs the risk that if the measure of the craft's utility is too great, then there will be tremendous pressure to join the minority which exercises it, and this minority in turn will have a considerable incentive to opt out of the maximal unit, to set up on its own, and establish a monopoly. If this happens the local society will not long remain organized according to the principle of mechanical solidarity.

This means that as u increases, then inevitably the population of the maximal economic unit, increases also, to the point that u does not have to be very large before this becomes equal to the number of the total population. Once this point is reached, u can still increase, to the point that p becomes very small indeed. If one considers the agricultural sector of an advanced economy (which is after all the only productive sector of the typical simple society), it is a very small fraction of the total economy. True, such an economy will also have an industrial sector, but in terms of social evolution, this is essentially derivative. But even taking every productive sector into account, p can still be very small, particularly in comparison with any simple agricultural economy.

p becomes small, because u becomes relatively larger, by continuously adding efficiency to the local economy, at a rate greater than the loss of population from the productive sector. Anthropology, traditionally, interested itself in societies for which p was nearly 1, and, therefore, $u = \mathcal{E}$. More and more this traditional sphere of interest confines anthropology to a narrow range of unimportant social systems, though it cannot be denied that the classic studies of simple societies established the theoretical basis for the development of the subject as a whole. But what happens when $u > \mathcal{E}$, and the questions as to how and why $u > \mathcal{E}$, constitute the main focus of current research. This must be the next stage of the present study.

COMPLEXITY, CLASS AND POVERTY

For the productive sector of any economy to be relatively small, a relatively large increase in efficiency must be contributed to it by the utility sector. But efficiency is also a factor within the utility sector, and not merely something which it exports to the productive sector. This situation creates something of a paradox. This can be demonstrated by taking a starting point where $u = u'$ and $p = p'$, and then introducing a small increment, η, in u, which could represent just that amount of growth in the craft sector of an economy, to the loss of the agricultural sector. This could mean that more people come to make ploughs, while fewer people use them, with the overall balance of advantage lying in increased production, in turn the result of more intensive ploughing. The objection to this analysis is that it is unreal, in that it does not represent the way in which—according to the records of history and ethnography—population shifts from the productive to the utility sector.

There is a perfectly logical reason for this. If total agricultural production remains constant, then an increase in the number of ploughs (and of the men who make them), can only mean that the output per plough declines, even though the output of every farmer must increase, so that they can maintain the total production, with their reduced numbers. This is contrary to all principles of economic efficiency and incentive: what demand can there be for a less efficient plough? The balance existing between the productive and utility sectors of an economy must represent a point of division between the two where the efficiency contribution from the utility sector to each individual producer is a maximum in relation to the demand for his products. This paradox can be resolved if η represents not more ploughs of the same sort, but a better plough—with no increase in the number produced. That is, the factor which increases the contribution of the utility sector is innovation, or in technological terms, invention. Innovation is, however, much wider than invention, since it can occur also in the realms of culture and social organization.

We live in a society which takes innovation for granted. The human societies which existed during the first million odd years of man's history (which ended only a little more than 10,000 years ago) hardly knew it at all. If one takes an isolated stone age people, such as the Tiwi of Bathurst island off Northern Australia,[9] all the evidence suggests that nothing in their way of life has changed in the course of thousands of years. There may have been minor changes in the vocabulary of their language, or in other types of symbolism, but these would have been no more than questions of detail.

Innovation inevitably adds to the complexity of any society. This is hardly more than a question of definition. If a new element is introduced into any unity, the result must be greater complexity, following inevitably from the new relations which must be established to integrate the new element into the existing whole.

This means that u does not gradually increase, and p gradually decrease—at least in broad historical terms—but that every increase, η, represents an innovation. At an elementary level, and for a given society, the first innovation can be represented by η_1, the second by η_2, and so on up to the most recent, say with successive increases in u, so that $u_1 = \eta_1$, $u_2 = \eta_1 + \eta_2$ and so on, up to $u_n = \eta_1 + \eta_2 + \ldots + \eta_n$. At this level every one of the n different η's can represent a different contribution of crafts or services by the utility to the production sector of the economy.

The first possibility for differentiation of classes within any economy occurred when man first took to cultivation and the herding of animals, the so-called neolithic revolution. This did not of itself require any such differentiation, and even today there are any number of neolithic peoples without any separate identifiable social class, corresponding to the utility sector of the economy. There are others where this sector exists, but is sub-divided among all the maximal economic units.[10] This could well be so with the first craft innovation, represented by η_1, which could well be weaving or pottery-making. But if, proceeding from one innovation to another, through η_2 to η_3 and so on, every one of them contributes more to the efficiency of the productive sector, than it takes away from the population actively engaged in this sector, the surplus production must at every stage become a higher proportion of the total production.

The use and application of surplus production is an aspect of all human social organization, for the reasons given in Chapter 4. The development of the u-sector does not have to proceed very far before it gets more than its fair share of the total production, which by definition comes from the p-sector. In strict evolutionary terms this need be no loss to the p-sector, since its share of total produce may still be higher than it would be without the added efficiency contributed by the u-sector.

It might be wondered why the p-sector does not hold out for a larger share. In purely economic terms the answer is that it lies at the mercy of the u-sector, which can always threaten paralysis by cutting off supplies. The fact that the u-sector has always developed out of successive innovations give it a sort of intellectual or cultural dominance over the p-sector. So also, as the u-sector breaks away from the social structures of the p-sector, which it tends to do at a comparatively early stage of development, it becomes well-placed to develop political institutions which protect its own special interests. The most original of these is the city, which in its Greek version, *polis*, provides the basic root for the English word, *political*. Within the city all the components $\eta_1, \eta_2, \ldots$ of the u-sector can have their own separate enclaves, to which admission can be severely restricted, say even to the sons of existing members. This is the rationale of the whole guild organization of medieval Europe, but it has its parallels in such classes as the Benin brass-smiths of Nigeria.[11] The unity of the city makes it admirably defensive, and further gives it the opportunity to use force to dominate the surrounding countryside.

Force itself may be judged in terms of economic utility, even though it may be a purely negative factor for cultivators whose fields are despoiled in war. So much is this so, that the class which has the command over force is a very special case of its own. In economic terms the ruling classes can be defined as that part of the u-sector which offers defensive values to all the economy, not on the basis of free exchange (for this would not be true to its nature), but by simple imposition. Indeed it cannot be too much emphasized that once the p-sector and the u-sector exist side-by-side, the p-sector has little choice about what it accepts from the u-sector, or about the terms of acceptance. The ruling classes are perhaps to be distinguished from other categories in the u-sector in that they work upon the p-sector primarily by means of political rather than economic sanctions, but then the difference between political and economic institutions is finer than it appears at first sight. Is slavery, for example, a political or an economic institution?

The characteristic agricultural sector of a class-differentiated society, of the kind which appears from the discussion above, is called a *peasantry*.[12] It is the characteristic rural society of the greater part of the third world, and is becoming more and more the centre of interest for anthropologists. There are two main reasons for this. The first is that peasant societies for the most part occupy marginal land which they work at a comparatively low level of technology. Since they largely stand apart from the u-sector of the total economy of which they are a part, they can, and indeed do, preserve many of the simpler social structures of earlier primitive populations. If a peasant society is looked at from within, it appears to be preoccupied with the production of its staple crop, subject always to a part of its production being contributed to the larger outside economy. That is, not all its surplus can be used for its own involutionary purposes. Indeed the utility contributed by the outside economy may so increase the surplus, that the peasant sector gains rather than loses from the relationship between the two. For an example of this, one need only consider the enormously increased efficiency which the Indian cultivators of middle America (for instance, the Chamulas) derive from the use of the *machete*, which they can acquire relatively cheaply in terms of their own production.

The second reason for the anthropologists' interest in peasants is that they represent the most important development problem in the third world. Peasants are becoming almost everywhere so numerous in relation to the lands which they have to cultivate, that the soil tends to be overworked, therefore becoming less productive, while at the same time, poor technology makes for a low output from every unit of labour. Better technology, however much it might

increase production, would lessen the demand for labour, and therefore accentuate the factor of over-population. This is happening all
over the third world, with the result that there are vast migrations
away from the countryside.[13] Peasant societies are often thought of
in association with a parasitical ruling class: the feudal manor,[14]
the Latin American latifundia,[15] the Italian mezzadria,[16] or even the
Indian caste system,[17] are commonly regarded as institutions for exploiting oppressed peasantry. The peasants themselves connote one
condition, more than any other, and that is poverty. True it is,
peasants are almost always poor, when it is a question of their share
of the produce of the total economy of which they are a part. It is
easy to think that all that need be done to alleviate this poverty is to
abolish these oppressive institutions. Such a reform has been adopted
in many areas—Italy, Mexico, India are only a few of the examples
—but it has proved no more than a partial solution. The fact is that
peasants would still be inefficient producers, even if they were free
to deal with their entire produce. In present terms their input from
the u-sector is much too small: their society is much too small: their
society is much too isolated to benefit from the utility which the
total economy has to offer. Agriculture can be efficient, but only on
terms incompatible with the fundamental structure of peasant
societies.

Migration to cities is a commonly adopted solution to peasant
economic problems. This means the movement of population from
the p-sector to the u-sector. The question then arises as to what it is
about the u-sector, which the p-sector lacks, that gives it the capacity
to absorb so many new constituent members. The u-sector, of its
very nature, is a complex amalgam of different sub-sectors, whose
contributions have been designated above in algebraic notation, as
$\eta_1, \eta_2 \ldots \eta_n$. There is no question of the sub-sectors having equal
weight, whether in terms of their input to the total economy, or of
the number of people engaged in each of them. With each sub-sector
connoting a different innovation, then plainly that devoted to the
money-based exchange of goods (or, briefly, *trade*) will contribute
beyond measure to the efficiency of a differentiated economy, even
though individual units may be poor and inefficient. No innovation
was ever so important as money, which immediately gives almost
unlimited capaciy for expansion to the distributive sector of any
economy.[18] This means that almost anyone who leaves the p-sector
can almost always find a niche in the u-sector, by constituting
himself as just one further link in the chain of distribution of some

class of products. The former peasant cultivator may be able to assume this new role without leaving the countryside, but in the end it is likely to mean moving to the city.[19] It is this process, for instance, which has made Mexico City the sixth largest city in the world; there one can see small traders almost beyond number, some operating from shops which are little more than a hole in the wall, others setting up stalls in back-streets, others selling newspapers, ball-point pens and chewing gum in the city's buses, the whole lot being supported by others who render petty services as shoe-shine boys, messengers and so on. The capacity for a convoluted distributive system to support a vast population is simply astonishing. It also opens up a whole new field of anthropological study. The distinctive urban institutions in this field have been summed up by the American anthropologist Oscar Lewis, under the heading of 'the culture of poverty'. His own studies,[20] carried out in Mexico City, reveal a world of highly unstable social groups, small in scale, with the only focal point the mother of the family, often abandoned by her husband and older children; this society, precarious and insecure, is constantly preoccupied by the search for any sort of transaction which will bring in money. Since the most profitable transaction of this kind is stealing, the culture of poverty is characterized by violence and mistrust among neighbours. This urban society may well benefit from modern technology in terms of bus services, electric light and so on, and may even enjoy some kind of public welfare, but it is marginal to the total economy. Indeed in countries such as Holland or England the culture of poverty is almost unknown, simply because there is no population residue which needs to be absorbed into the distributive sector under this category. At the most it may characterize a few immigrant groups such as the Sikhs of Coventry, or the Bengalis of the East End of London. In the United States the Puerto Ricans in New York, or the Chicanos of the West Coast, constitute such a culture, but in almost every case these are essentially foreign or racial minorities, however much we may condemn the political system which allows them to exist in such penury.[21]

To remedy the ills which characterize the culture of poverty, or which plague any impoverished peasantry, one must look further to other economic institutions, particularly those of the capitalist economies of the Western world, to see what is missing. Peasants and the urban poor, and the classes which exploit them, may make up almost the whole of society, in many parts of the world, but they do not add up to a complete picture. At this stage the element of capital is imperfectly represented: without it no political or economic analysis is complete. The meaning of capital, particularly in its social dimension, must therefore constitute the final section of this chapter.

SAVING, INVESTMENT AND CAPITAL

The economic systems considered in the first two sections of this chapter, however elaborate they may be, depend upon the continuous application of production to immediate consumption needs. The fact that the elaboration of these systems takes the form of a highly convoluted distributive network does no more than separate consumption from production by a chain whose links consist of a large number of very small-scale transactions. Very little is set aside from current production, to provide for the future, and what is set aside, such as the seed corn for the new-year's sowing, is only so much as is needed to maintain production at current levels, allowing perhaps for some increase to take population growth into account.

Even at an elementary level, some production must be of enduring assets, from the bow and arrows used by the primitive hunter, to the artifacts to be found in the average neolithic household. So also, a population does not have to be very advanced before it builds permanent dwellings for itself. Wear and tear limits the life of all these assets, so that even if they last longer than one annual production cycle, production can still continue on an annual basis. For to the potter who produces a water-jug which last for five years, the output to be maintained is precisely the same as it would be if the water-jug lasted for only one year, but had to be produced for a population of only one-fifth of the size. Even when money comes into the equation, it is seldom retained for a period longer than a year; credit, where it is granted, is limited in the same way, generally to the time of the next harvest, when funds become available for the repayment of debts. The position was not much changed by the beginnings of international maritime trade, when the time limit for credit was based on the expected time for a cargo to arrive at a home port.[22] Even today a vast amount of the business done in international money markets depends on three- and six-month credits.

The production of goods depends upon a number of so-called 'factors in production', which comprehend all contributions to the productive process, labour, raw materials, and so on. Now in the common case of a peasant agricultural economy, which sells its surplus production for distribution throughout the larger total economy, few of the factors in production have themselves to be acquired by purchase. True, in modern conditions, peasants tend to buy tools, clothing, and small consumer durables such as wrist-watches, but this is a recent, and inessential development. Tradition-ally the exchange which comes into a peasant economy, if it is not mopped up by a parasitical dominant class, generates its own sphere of activity, such as the frequent and elaborate celebrations of religious feasts by the Indians of Central America.[23] The critical point is that little or none of this exchange can be devoted to in-creasing the size or efficiency of any productive unit, since the two critical factors in agricultural production, land and labour, are not within the exchange economy, that is, in monetary terms, they are not for sale. Such arrangements as exist for one man to help out another, particularly on a relatively large-scale and long-term operation such as building a house, often provide for the help to be given on a mutual basis, and if it is remunerated, it will only be in terms of local produce, such as grain or alcohol in prescribed amounts.

A similar analysis could be made of the corresponding urban distributive sector of the total economy, such as the Mexico City of Oscar Lewis, noting that what this economy produces is not the goods which it distributes, but the utility represented by the service of distribution. Here too land and labour are not within the ex-change economy of the sector itself (although they are naturally exchange goods in the total economy). The importance of this, in terms of the development of economic institutions, is that there is no scope, let alone incentive, to establish efficient large-scale enterprises, where access to two essential factors, land and labour, does not exist. There is a political as well as an economic dimension to this: it is no accident, for instance, that the armies of feudal Europe were unpaid, and disbanded after almost every battle. The employment of so-called 'mercenaries' occurred at a much later stage, and rep-resents a distinct economic advance.

In the economies so far considered, every unit is static, inefficient and small in scale, and any particular sector is comprised by a multiplicity of similar units of this character. The economic unit is static, or more precisely homeostatic, not so much because it has no surplus production to apply to its own expansion and develop-ment, but simply because the constraints of the situation in which it operates give it no incentive to do so. Even if it could become more efficient without adding to its existing factors in production, this would not necessarily give it any greater share of the market. If, therefore, surplus production is to be turned to development, the constraints must be substantially relaxed. For this to happen, there must be a governing class, already having a substantial interest in the two critical factors of land and labour, which becomes so convinced of the benefits which more efficient production will bring to itself, that it will use its power to this end. This is asking a good deal, since this class will already, as landlords, have more than its fair share of the produce of the total economy. Even at the top there is not always incentive for innovation and development.

In fact the break-through, generally known as the industrial revolution, originated in but one country, England, from which it spread throughout the world. How and why this happened are questions for economic history.[24] The anthropologist is interested in the new economic institutions which arose, and the new social structures which developed in line with them.

On the purely institutional side, the fundamental innovation came from the application of surplus, to improvements in and extensions of the productive unit. That is production could be saved and invested, with the use of money playing an important part in this process. The improvements took the form of assets, such as power-driven machinery, of unprecedented scale and efficiency. Expansion was possible, because everything needed for it, particularly land and labour was at last in the market. The accumulated wealth represented by such expansion and improvement is known as capital. It could be valued in monetary terms according to the production invested in building it up. The need for new investment could well run ahead of the cash-flow retained from sales, creating a crisis in liquidity which special monetary institutions, notably the banks, could help resolve by making long-term loans at interest. As an enterprise grew in scale, the original participants (or their successors) might no longer be able to manage and finance it by themselves, and so new participation would be invited, by subscription of cash for further development, in exchange for a share of the future profits. At the same time a new class of managers grew up, bureaucrats remunerated by fixed salaries, to share the management burdens of the proprietors.[25] This class itself made its own contribution in terms of professional competence and efficiency, and rapidly became a major factor in production, to the point that the large-scale enterprises of the present time show a complete divorce between owners and managers. This has required purely institutional innovations, such as that of the joint-stock company, incorporated with limited liability, at many stages of development—and every new such institution adds to the complexity of the whole economy, requiring whole new classes of functionaries to maintain it.

Industry is the characteristic economic enterprise based upon large-scale fixed assets, generally organized into a factory, with the necessary energy for production not provided primarily by human labour: indeed, although the first industrial revolution had its beginnings in the agricultural sector, it was not long before the process of power-driven manufacture, using the steam-engine, developed. Nor must it be thought that the population was transformed into an army of bureaucrats and managers: the labour displaced in the countryside by the adoption of improved methods of agriculture, was largely taken up in factory production in the cities, as an undifferentiated unskilled mass, in which all every man had to sell, and that in competition with all others like him, was the use of his own body as a factor in production. The same was true of the labour engaged in primary production, in the mines, which enormously expanded to meet the new demands of industry for their products, or even in the countryside where a residue survived to maintain the essential agricultural sector. These constitute the proletariat, so essential in Marx's political economy.

This is a whole new area for anthropological research. In the third world, the area which most interests the anthropologists, the proletariat is still imperfectly developed. In many areas, industry is only just beginning, and the exchange sector of the economy tends still to be based on mines and plantations, which often rely on transient migrant labour, imported from the highly traditional agricultural sector. Peasants are often constrained to work on distant plantations for several months of the year: the Chamulas for instance go down to the coffee *fincas* of Chiapas' Pacific coast. Africa, in particular, provides numerous examples of the organization of local rural societies being affected, often radically, by the temporary absence of many of their men in distant mines.[26] It has already been demonstrated, that where land shortage has forced permanent migration, this is often to large capital cities, and that the new society established is not strictly an industrial proletariat, but is more a case of 'the culture of poverty'. There is some correspondence between the two, and twentieth-century Mexico City can to some degree be equated with nineteenth-century London, but there are important differences, too, particularly in the prospects for future development.

The most significant consequence of economic complexity, and the vast diversity of role and function which goes with it, is the emergence of any number of partial social systems, partial not only in that each one comprises a mere fraction of the total population, but also in the sense it demands only a part of the time of its constituent members. In the purely productive sphere, the processes of modern factory production have become so complex, and the factors in production so diverse, that in terms of function the industrial society becomes utterly fragmented, to the point that no part of it has any but an incidental interest in the final product, which in many cases will not even be intended for ordinary domestic use. This created the condition of *alienation*, with imponderable social consequences.[27] The modern factory worker can well find all his leisure, proceeding automatically through his hours on the production line of the factory which employs him.[28] White-collar workers can react in the same way, for what each lacks is any opportunity for strategy. Here the !Kung bushman, the Bemba, the Trobriander or the Chamula, to cite but a few of the pre-industrial peoples already mentioned are immeasurably better off. Even the urban poor of the third world, with their culture of poverty, share something of this advantage. One need not be a social psychologist to see how significant it is that so much working-class leisure is devoted to activities, such as gambling, which contains this missing element of strategy, of making decisions affecting future action.

This analysis can well end with the suggestion that the fundamental division in the society of a modern industrial state is based upon this element, with those whose economic occupations contain it, differing markedly from the rest, in their way of life, their social organization, their systems of values and so on, according to every variable which can characterize a social system. Here is immense scope for future study and research, but it will be outside the traditional areas of anthropological interest, as much as it is beyond the range of the present chapter.

6

Morality, Law and the Settlement of Disputes

There is nothing either good or bad, but thinking makes it so.

Hamlet II ii.

Morality is a way of thinking according to which all human actions are judged. The judgement itself is polarized between right and wrong. It is concerned with the quality, and not the substance of the action. It takes into consideration the motives, the circumstances—and particularly in primitive cultures—the consequences of the action. The basic proposition of morality in any popular culture is 'there is a right and a wrong way of doing everything'.

The practical problem in enforcing morality is that moral issues are almost always too pervasive. This follows from the fact that in the education of the individual, from earliest childhood, each everyday action is presented in moral terms. A child is brought up to think that eating peas off a knife, or swearing, or causing injury to another, are all wrong: and it is in fact difficult for the young child to get the degree and kind of 'wrongness' into perspective. But what he will probably never appreciate (unless he becomes a social anthropologist) is that everything to do with morality is a matter of culture. There are in fact profound differences in the moral outlooks of different peoples. The normal man disregards this fact and applies his own moral standards in judging any 'foreigner'. So where an Englishman thinks a Spaniard cruel to animals, the Spaniard thinks the Englishman cruel to children. It is pointless to argue the rights and wrongs of a question such as this in cosmic terms. It is much better to get to know the parts played by animals and children in the respective cultures, and to see how the different moral rules then govern them.

Morality is the rationale of behaviour in any culture. Since, ideally, culture is stable, morality is traditional and conformist. The moral ideal is essentially homeostatic; people should do no more than continue to behave in the way that they always have—at least in the ideal conception of their past behaviour. Accepting that approved types of behaviour in any society are not disfunctional (for if they were, they would not continue), it must be true of a practice obnoxious to us, such as the gratuitous killings which are essential for a Kalinga of the Northern Philippines to achieve the status of a 'Pangat' (a sort of judge) that its social consequences, in its own context, are beneficial.[1] Our concern for the Pangat's victims is sentimental rather than scientific.

Morality, like any other aspects of culture, is generally enforced simply because it is accepted—as a result largely of education directed to this end—in every society. It is intrusive in the sense that any breach of a moral rule provokes some reaction, even if it is unobserved. This, in a trivial case, such as a breach of table manners, is likely to be no more than ridicule. In other cases the reaction will be more serious, and here there is a parting of the ways, with one way leading to religion, and the other to law.

The next chapter shows how almost any event in primitive experience is controlled by supernatural forces. Now an event may be seen as good or bad according to its social consequences interpreted in the light of culture. An abundant harvest is good; a poor one is bad. Too many deaths occurring at one time is bad; unseasonable weather is bad, and so on. Every event has its cause, which, by one means or another, is identified with human action. So the equation is that a 'good' event follows from a 'right' action, and a 'bad' event from a 'wrong' action. Moral judgements are therefore continuously being forced upon the primitive community, particularly because 'bad' events constantly recur.

In primitive thought it is the event which determines the action which caused it, which in turn decides the counteraction to be taken. So the *bad* event of a poor harvest with the Tallensi, means the *wrong* action of the local clan in failing in the rites of their ancestor cult, which may be put right by a prescribed sacrifice at the local ancestor shrine.[2]

In this case all the relevant factors are esoteric. But the Nyakyusa of Tanzania will attribute a 'poor' harvest to their 'divine' king, the Lwembe, and their counteraction may be to have him killed, rather painfully, by his retinue of priests.[3] Indeed it is common enough to attribute ill fortune to chiefly misrule, and to act accordingly.

Now the 'religious' response to moral situations will give way to the 'legal', the more the original 'wrong' action, the 'bad' event which follows it, and the counteraction then taken, focus upon particular individuals, and are worked out, systematically, in the 'physical' rather than the 'metaphysical' realm. Zande witchcraft, for instance, remains religious rather than legal, because only the 'bad' event, that is the sickness or death allegedly caused by the witchcraft, is actually physical.[4] This does not make the wrong action 'causing' this event, or the counteraction taken (which may in turn 'cause' another 'bad' event), any less real for the Azande.

Closer to the 'legal' process of the criminal trial is the poison ordeal of the Bushong of Zaire: here a particular woman is accused of having killed by witchcraft; the weighing of the evidence, followed as may be by conviction and sentence, are all achieved by the administration of a special poison, together with an oath in these terms: 'If you are guilty, you will die; if not, you will be saved.' The law exacts its toll, as with any judicial execution following a criminal trial. In legal terms the Bushong poison ordeal is very incomplete. The alleged crime is never made specific, and the procedure adopted bypasses any question of evidence in coming to judgement. Moreover its importance to the Bushong is social rather than legal: they are intent upon ridding their community of a source of impurity, which their experience shows adversely to have affected their welfare.[5] (This idea of impurity is reflected in the Judge's traditional nosegay in English murder trials).

The religious element tends to persist in all criminal law, whose sanctions are readily interpreted in terms of preventing the contamination of society by impure elements. Even a tribe such as the Cheyenne of the great American plains, who have an advanced criminal procedure, ensuring the trial of any case according to the evidence, see murder essentially in terms of social contamination.[6] For this reason, not only must the murderer be banished, but, at the same time, the sacred arrows of the tribe must be ritually renewed. The counteraction to any 'bad' event following a 'wrong' action is essentially social: this is because the original 'action' was antisocial, which in practice means not conforming to the traditions of the tribe. These will be grounded in its mythology, and preserved and enhanced by its rituals. In this light, morality is seen as human by endowment, social by practice, and cosmic by origin.

LAW AND SOCIETY

If morality is a way of thinking about human behaviour, law is a means of controlling it for the benefit of society. Its ends are practical rather than esoteric: it is concerned with 'order', that is the preservation of certain patterns of behaviour which experience shows as necessary for the general well-being of society. Now what the law seeks to preserve is the way in which people generally behave in respect to each other. Here there is a conflict between the actual and the ideal. The two are interrelated, and there is a constant feedback between them. For if conflicts between actual and ideal standards of behaviour in any society were too frequent, social control would break down. Essentially, therefore, the study of primitive law is a study of primitive behaviour focused on the instances where a dispute arises because of an alleged deviation from the ideal. These cases have a similar relation to law as rites do to religion. That is, the law continuously operates, but one can only see what it amounts to by studying the cases, which are the counteraction of society to deviations from the norms which govern it. But these norms are in turn defined by types of behaviour in the society, of which even deviant behaviour is a part. Law and order arise out of the very processes which they govern.

There is a danger in thinking of primitive law in terms of our own legal institutions. This led Evans-Pritchard to say of the Nuer, 'In a strict sense they have no law',[7] since they have no courts to adjudicate, nor any means of enforcing judgement.[8] This is a sterile approach, if it fails to recognize the true nature of primitive institutions of social control. It is then only too easy to see primitive law either as slavish adherence to custom, or as an inadequate means of restraining licence. In practice a preliterate society cannot easily systematize its law, which tends therefore to lack the coherence of modern legal systems, running at the same time to a multiplicity of specialized rules, inherently in conflict with each other. This does not mean, to quote Malinowski,[9] that primitive law consists of 'lengthy litanies of threaded statement, which makes us anthropologists look silly, and the savage look ridiculous'. One can go too far in the other direction, and see primitive law as explicable in terms only of the primitive culture: but this makes nonsense of social anthropology as a comparative science. What one can find is an essential unity about the law of a primitive society, but expressed in different categories to our own.

Primitive culture is concerned with the definition of status: a reading of this book so far will have made this clear. Every individual has a status, which is the totality of the ways in which he is regarded by his society, and by particular members of it. A child is seen as having special attributes, probably not much differentiated according to sex, which will be changed for others quite different on initiation into adulthood, whereupon status becomes very much dependent upon sex. Some of the attributes of the individual will be strictly relative: the status of a Tallensi mother's brother will only relate to that of his sister's sons.[10] There is also the special status of certain personalities in the local society, such as chiefs, priests or elders. And since poor communications tend to make for a small-scale society, the pattern of relationships between different individuals, which is what social life consists of, will be largely determined by the status ascribed to each one of them. A legal relationship is seen in terms of rights and obligations, and in a primitive society this relationship between two individuals will be determined by who they happen to be, that is, according to their status. The closer they are together, socially, the more the relationship will affect many different aspects of their lives. In our own society one sees this within the immediate family circle, but hardly at all outside it, except, significantly, in the individual's relationship with bureaucracy. In a primitive society the extent of relationships prescribed by status is much greater, which explains why so many of their legal institutions are so different from our own.

Status is imposed by the conventions of the local society: no individual can do much to change this. For an advanced society status is a much less important concept, but it may be *achieved*,[11] that is, acquired by the exertions of the individual. In primitive society the area of choice in the life of the individual is very small. There may be no chance of economic enterprise, and circumstances may often determine even the choice of one's spouse. It is as if one was always playing a part in a play. In an advanced society, by contrast, one may enter at will into all kinds of different relationships, most of them very short-lived, and entirely trivial: one need only compare the difference between the shopper in a modern supermarket, and a women who has bought a load of goods in a Tiv market.[12] The supermarket range of goods is enormous, the identity of the individual shoppers means nothing to the proprietors, and the relationship between them is utterly transient. This is the essence of the modern law of contract. The Tiv market is an institution affecting many different aspects of day to day life: only a narrow range of goods will be exchanged, over a relatively small number of transactions. But the people in the market will be related to each other by all kinds of ties, and the market will be the place for working out any number of different relationships—including, as one might expect, the settlement of disputes.

Disputes are grist to the mill of any system of law. Without them there would be no litigation, and no establishment of a legal tradition, or a rule of precedent, to use the legal term. They arise in a primitive community because relationships based on status are too constructing, or too ambiguous. Where the traditional regulation of marriage is too severe, there is likely to be adultery, as witness the Tiwi of Northern Australia where most of the young women are married to very old men.[13] Where the kinship rules which determine the village chief may, by varying interpretations of the facts, lead to different results, then there will be disputes about succession. Where a quite inadequate number of cattle exist to pay the prescribed sums in bridewealth, there are likely to be disputes about the ownership of cattle, or, indeed, the ownership of women as wives or daughters. It is of the nature of man sometimes to disobey the rules, and the resolution of conflict may itself be an important part of the mechanism of social control.

It follows, in such a case, that the dispute can seldom be limited to a single issue between two individuals. Such an issue is much more likely to be a stage in a conflict over all kinds of different, but related issues, between the two largest separate groups of which the individuals are members. The conflict may focus on one particular issue, such as unpaid bridewealth, but this need be little more than a legal fiction upon which all other issues may turn. This is very much the case with the Lakeside Tonga of Malawi, for whom litigation of this kind provides the forum for the resolution of most of their political problems.[14]

These disputes are part of what we would call the *civil*, as opposed to the *criminal* law. The distinction has not the same force in primitive law, and is blurred by all kinds of attitudes which are far from our own thinking. Thus the Dinka sees the loss of a man by homicide, or of a woman by marriage, as both requiring payment in cattle.[15] This is because cattle for the Dinka are the basic measure of any important interest, as Chapter 3 shows. This fundamental element in a system of law may be expressed in more abstract terms, such as the Injô of the Tiv,[16] or the Hka of the

Kachin,[17] which are often translated as *debt*. They represent no more than the obligation of one party to the other in a dispute. The Tiv see any deviation from the law as 'spoiling the Tar', the Tar being the basic unit at any level in their kinship and residence structure. Injô is the symbol and measure of this deviation: it can be loosely equated to the damages claimed in an English civil action, but its scope is far wider, and the idea of restoration has an element of public welfare more appropriate, by our standards, to the criminal law. This, in turn, in primitive societies, falls partly within the province of religion, as the first part of this chapter illustrates. This demonstrates once again the essential unity of the institutions of primitive society. The next part of this chapter will develop this point, by showing all the different parts which such institutions, of every kind, may play in the maintenance and enforcement of the law.

LEGAL INSTITUTIONS

A legal dispute in a modern state, if not previously settled by negotiation and agreement between the parties, or their representatives, will proceed to trial before a court, whose officials will have the power to enforce whatever judgement they come to. The court will allow—indeed encourage—the parties to be represented by advocates, and it will make such findings of fact as may be necessary by assessing evidence given by witnesses. The whole of its procedure, and the law which it enforces, will be authoritatively recorded in writing, and will be accessible as much to any member of the public, at least if properly instructed, as to the court itself. This is the common pattern of the administration of justice in any state with the necessary political and cultural resources, of which perhaps the most essential will be the written or printed word.

The institutions of primitive law inevitably deviate from this pattern at every turn: it provides, none the less, a useful model for studying them. Any plaintiff is more interested in obtaining a remedy for the wrong he claims to have suffered, than in the actual legal procedure, which this involves. The procedure serves only to obtain the remedy, although the costs and difficulties of any particular procedure, may make the remedy not worth pursuing; it is remarkable how at every level of human society this factor is disregarded. But in a primitive community none but the most simple procedure may exist—and within certain social relationships, the simpler the better. Thus the Crow Indians, who are organized in matrilineal clans, recognize a 'joking' relationship between a man and the sons of his father's clan—which would, of course, not be his own. The man may then be publicly ridiculed by his 'father's sons' for many different offences: this was a recognized sanction for good behaviour, rather than a remedy for a civil wrong.[18]

The practice can be extended so that a contest of 'insult songs' takes place between the kin-groups of the two parties in dispute, as the means of seeing whether the plaintiff's claim against the defendant succeeds. This the Tiv called 'drumming the scandal'[19], but it is no easier to judge the winner of such a contest, than it is to try the original case. It is not surprising that the Tiv song contests often led to a fight between the parties. But the song contest does have the practical advantage of translating the matter at issue into a more stereotyped form of contest. That is, there need be fewer rules for judging song-contests than for trying disputed issues of fact and law. To the primitive mind, also, it is quite to be expected that the party in the right, with the support of his kin, should sing the best songs.

This way of trying disputes may also take the form of the competitive destruction of wealth, such as is practised by the Apa Tanis of central India.[20] This lets off a lot of steam, and is very face-saving. The richest party may win, but that is probably best for the stability of the local society. It may be, though, that a group which has lately acquired considerable wealth will pick a quarrel, just so as to resolve it, to their own social and political advancement, in this way.

Often a dispute leads to the start, or more often, the revival of a feud, between the different political or kinship groups which the parties belong to. This is common practice with the Nuer, especially between villages in the same district. The usual incident in the feud is homicide, and this carries with it a ritual means for finally resolving the dispute. For the killer must immediately visit a leopard-skin chief, who cuts his arm so that blood flows. He may stay with the chief for sanctuary. At the same time the chief summons the dead man's kin to see whether they will accept cattle in compensation. If this is agreed to, the chief collects cattle from the killer's kin, and takes them to the dead man's home, where he makes certain prescribed sacrifices.[21]

The leopard-skin chief is hardly a judge, since he has no power to enforce his ruling. He provides the ritual means for sealing an agreement which ends a dispute. This is a common enough institution of primitive law: the Comanche peace-chief has the power to seal the settlement of a dispute with his peace-pipe.[22] In some societies the settlement will be ratified by the holding of a feast: the sharing of a common board is often of great ritual and symbolic meaning for primitive peoples. This explains why a feast is often given, as by the Cheyenne, to reintroduce a returned exile, say one banished for homicide, into the tribe.[22]

It is the weakness of judicial personnel which so limits the enforcement of primitive law. There is too seldom a third person with the right power and authority. Sometimes a disinterested third party will intervene, such as the Comanche champion, who does apparently have authority to enforce his decisions. This authority is often ambiguous: with the Pangat of the Kalingas it is more a question of prestige gained from successful head-hunting expeditions, but this carries considerable weight.[23] Judgement is often best enforced where it is recognized as the concern of a definite group, such as the Tiv officials known as Mbatarev, who exist in every Tar. They are convened *ad hoc* to form a *jir*, which means both the court and the case which it tries.[24] So also, with the Arusha, of Tanzania, the parish elders, who form the local government, also try disputes.[25] This is very important in political control. The Alur chiefs of Uganda, mentioned in Chapter 3, were esteemed for their judicial powers, which were the envy of their neighbours.[26] At the top end of the scale are a people such as the Lozi of Zambia, whose judges have all the authority necessary to intervene in disputes, enforce their decisions, adduce evidence, and so on.[27]

This last question of evidence is often where primitive legal institutions are weakest. Witnesses present considerable problems to any court, and evidence is often the weakest link in trial procedure. The particular claim of the Kalinga Pangat was to discover the truth of any cause. But his methods were certainly unscientific, and elsewhere, also, the discovery of truth is left to diviners and keepers of oracles. Even simpler is the oath sworn by the parties, as on a Cheyenne peace-pipe, which carries the supernatural sanction that anyone who has sworn falsely will suffer some grievous misfortune, even to the point of the death of himself or a member of his family. This combines evidence, judgement and sentence in one operation: this is true of other primitive forms of trial, such as the Bushong poison ordeal, described in the first part of this chapter.[28] By our standards it may be arbitrary: it is certainly effective.

Against this background one would hardly expect to find legislation, that is the making of new law in abstract terms, without any reference to any one particular case. Yet a few instances are recorded. The first, from the Cheyenne, followed a case of borrowing a horse without permission: the borrower left a bow-and-arrow for security, and the military society of the elk-soldiers which tried the case, held that this exonerated him. But the difficulties inherent in the case were such that the elk-soldiers *legislated* in categorical terms that in the future there should be no horse-borrowing without permission.[29]

A quite different instance, from the Labwor of Uganda, shows legislation brought in to meet a new political situation. The tribe's cattle were being killed by their neighbours, the Achole, who had come to own guns. The Labwor elders, therefore, ritually killed one of their own cows, and buried it, at the same time pronouncing a formal ban on anyone keeping cattle. It was foreign colonization which enabled the Achole to get their guns, and in the course of time this was to change the whole position of primitive peoples.[30] There was superimposed upon their tribal law all the legal institutions of the colonizing power, including a complete and authoritative judicial and legislative procedure. These included all the bureaucratic apparatus described in Chapter 3, although special problems arose when those with traditional authority had to adapt to bureaucratic roles.[31] The legal basis of a bureaucracy inevitably incorporates extensive legislative powers, and the more bureaucratic control is extended, the more these powers are made use of, and the more restricted is the scope of traditional law. The process is a very gradual one, and even today, the Anglo-American common law, which is a traditional legal system based entirely on a rule of precedent, is a major part of the legal corpus of the countries of the English-speaking world. The application of the common law is for the most part confined to actions between individuals, whereas cases involving government departments or giant corporations tend to turn on legislation. Many legal systems have a special branch of the law governing the operation of the bureaucracy, both as a self-contained corporation, and in its relations with the general public: such is the French *droit administratif*.

A legal system is a good historical model of social and political structure. The fact that such a system is of its nature liable to focus on disputes does not matter. The character of any social structure is refracted by the conflicts inherent in it, however stable it may be. Indeed conflict-analysis is a common approach to anthropological problems.[32] The use of law as a model also has the advantage that changes are gradual, and well-documented: the disadvantage is that law is essentially public, and reveals little about the private events in human life—so long, at least, as they remain outside the area of dispute. The answer is that for a complete picture of any social system, it must be looked at from many different perspectives, each one legitimate, but none complete.

7

Communication and Culture

However culture is defined it is essentially something which man acquires as a member of society. Now the culture of all and every society is so complex, that its whole existence can only be sustained by a system—or better systems—of communication far more elaborate than could exist in any purely natural order. It is as a 'communicating' species that man is essentially different from all other living creatures.

The essence of human communication is the 'sign': so much is this so, that there is a whole new science of 'seminology'—from the Greek *semeion*, a 'sign'—which has developed from the ideas of the French scholar, Ferdinand de Saussure.[1] A sign has a *form* and a *content*. The *form* of an audible sign, is what is sounds like, and of a visible sign, what it looks like. The *content* of a sign is what it means. The form *signifies*; the content is *signified*. A sign is the union between its form and its content, but the essence of a sign is purely conventional, arbitrary and extrinsic. The form of a sign never of itself discloses its content: the link between the two must always be learnt. This is not to say that the usefulness of a sign is necessarily independent of its form. Take, for example, a ship's fog-horn. This is a sign: its form is its loud distinctive monotone, its content is the message that the ship is somewhere in the immediate neighbourhood. Theoretically, at least, the same message could be communicated—by recognized convention—by having the ship's orchestra play 'Pop goes the weasel', but the unsuitability of this form for the relevant content need hardly be laboured.

Now the *form* of the fog-horn is so much determined by its *content*, that it has almost become a 'symbol'. What, then, is the difference between a symbol and a sign, at least as these words are best used in semiology or linguistics, and in this book as well? One aspect of the distinction is that a symbol by its form essentially discloses a part at least of its content. The international 'road-signs' are an interesting collection of forms, which—on this understanding—run the gamut from sign to symbol. The 'form' marking the end of a speed-limit ⊘ is substantially a *sign*, although a life-long process of acculturation may incline us to think of it as a symbol. The 'unguarded level-crossing' 🚂 is much more a symbol, since it portrays what is recognizably a train. The road signs comprise therefore a common code, which is at one level a mixed code of signs and symbols. This is a fairly common property of *visual* codes, including such examples as the hand-language used by Trappist monks to communicate with each other.

It is useful, however, to regard these codes as consisting of signs rather than symbols. The reason is that a symbol not only discloses a part at least of its content, but goes far beyond this disclosure so as to encapsulate a whole train of ideas, for which it is the starting point. A really condensed symbol has a whole 'cosmology' behind it. It may also convey its meaning in isolation, whereas essentially signs depend on their place in a whole interrelated system.

This introduction makes it possible to look at language as a social and cultural phenomenon, which is how an anthropologist sees it. For language, and most particularly spoken language, is the system of signs *par excellence*. Hardly a single word, let alone a sentence, in any language, has any intrinsic meaning. You could look at the word 'przyjaciel' for hours, calling in every mystical aid to contemplation and revelation, without realizing that it was the Polish for 'friend'. There is no reason why it should be so, except that it is. Its ancestry in the Slavonic, and ultimately the whole corpus of Indo-European languages could no doubt be traced, but at the end of the day nothing would be achieved, save relating this word to other 'signs' equally without intrinsic meaning. And it would be hopeless to pursue any theory, such as that it represented the sound of one friend embracing another. Any such naturalistic theory leads nowhere: even dogs, cows and Rice-Crispies, make different noises in France or Germany. The form-content relationship at every level, and in every language, is entirely arbitrary. Language represents the ultimate irreducibility of the cultural to the natural order. The fact that form is independent of content means that the range of possible different languages is almost unlimited.

The raw material used in the construction of almost every known language consists of the sounds which our tongues, vocal chords, larynxes and so on—which together comprise the human speech mechanism—may produce. There are curiosities such as the perfectly complete whistled language of Mazateco[2] men (though not women) in Southern Mexico, but these are subordinate to spoken languages directly related to them. Babbling babies can produce an astonishing range of sounds, which by the earliest process of education can be focused into speech patterns of any known language.

In practice this process is directed towards the end of the child acquiring the language of its own family. The result is to suppress the use of the majority of the sounds that the child, physically speaking, can make, and to enhance the use of the remaining minority. Psychologically the process is so effective that from a very early age one finds it difficult, if not impossible, to make the sounds of any language but one's own. And the narrow range of sounds of one's own language will contain nuances undetectable by 'foreigners'. Compare, for instance, the pronunciation of the English words, 'hare', 'heir', 'here' and 'hear'. In pure theory a language could be contructed out of any part, however restricted, of the spectrum of sound produced by the human speech mechanism.

The significant units of sound are called 'phonemes': they are the fundamental raw material of language. To communicate anything sensible they must be combined together according to certain recognized rules of word formation, syntax and grammar. The sentence rather than the word is the basic unit of language regarded as a means of communication. Here again there is a further sifting process, for only a very small part of the possible combinations of phonemes convey meaning in any given language, whether at the level of the word or the sentence. All the rules must be kept for language to serve its only true purpose of communication, as Lewis Carroll illustrated by his 'Jabberwockey':

> 'Twas brillig, and the slithy toves
> Did gyre and gimble in the wabe
> All mimsy were the borogroves,
> And the mome raths outgrabe.[3]

This is recognizably English rather than any other language, since it contains more of the essential forms of English, and yet being devoid of meaning (save in a very esoteric sense) it is strictly not language at all. It is inspired babbling of a professional mathematician.

There is a temptation to see a language as a model of any society which speaks it: this is a mistaken idea. Although it is intuitively difficult to dissociate the English from the English language—the tongue which Shakespeare spake, and so on—there is no essential connection between the two. English, like any other language, does happen to be a perfect and complete medium of spoken communication among English people, but very few adaptations would be necessary for any other language to play this role. This may be speculative, since a proposition of this kind is next to impossible to verify experimentally. But there are enough examples of cultural diversity within a common language, or of linguistic diversity within a common culture,[4] for it to be clear that no language needs an essential cultural basis apart from itself: that is, viewed as a cultural system, any language has almost complete autonomy.

This is not to say that the language of a particular people will not reflect their loyal environment. One may contrast for instance the extraordinary wealth of the Bemba language in regard to trees, with its poverty in regard to flowers.[5] From this certain facts about Bemba culture may be deduced. But if a wave of conquest were to leave the Bemba speaking some new language, this too would immediately adapt itself to embrace all the necessary concepts relating to trees—provided at least that the Bemba culture otherwise remained intact.

The multiplicity of the world's different languages allows few generalizations as to what is essential in the structure of any language. The pursuit of a *grammaire générale*, once much favoured by French scholars,[6]—and now by the American' Chomsky—has been largely inconclusive[7]. It is surprising how many apparently essential grammatical forms are lacking in languages other than one's own.

There is no question, now, of one language being more advanced than another. The language of the most primitive stone age culture in Africa is no more closely related to the chattering of baboons than is modern English. Primitive peoples no more talk baby talk than we do ourselves. Nor can one identify any general linguistic trends, whether towards greater simplicity, or greater complexity. Almost any line of development can be discovered in individual cases, which prove nothing in the general case.

The social significance of language for man is too obvious to need any further emphasis. It is the primary means whereby the individual is integrated into the culture of his own community. It is both the product and the instrument of that culture. Man is a slave to his language, which is more or less arbitrarily determined for him by the circumstances of his childhood. Yet certain men, as they grow up, see the way to make their former master their slave. Not only can they add to their language, but they can so use it as to add to their own power and influence in society. This use of language is relatively rare in the more primitive societies preferred by the anthropologist: it is common enough in our own. In any society it must be some process of this kind which leads to the evolution of language—such as history abundantly records. Such *mastery* of language, and its various possible consequences, are recognizable phenomena.[8]

More generally any society conceives the world as built up of the language habits of its members. Thinking is essentially linguistic. It is this which enables all the abstraction of ideas, whether in the fields of kinship, economics or religion, whereby man extends the control of his own culture over himself. Even the simplest human cosmology could not be communicated without language. Now this process of abstraction has gone so far as to enable special languages to be constructed which talk about nothing but themselves. Such is the language of pure mathematics: it makes up for the narrowness of its content by the extent of its range, which among the *cognoscenti* (who otherwise need have nothing in common) is worldwide.

The modern world is full of such meta-languages; they are only made possible by writing, and even more, printing, which are in no way essential to language as speech. They depend only a little on actual language: one would not, for instance, have to learn much Hungarian to understand a Hungarian chess magazine. On the other hand it would be essential to have learnt chess.

All these factors combine to make possible the application of the scientific method to the study of language, in a way not possible with any other aspect of culture. The precision and regularity, certainty and definiteness of a language are at the same level, intellectually, as the same qualities for the natural sciences. Historically the systematic study of language preceded any similar treatment of science: the medieval grammarians were essential forerunners of the scientists of the 'enlightenment'. But as seen by an anthropologist, language study is no more than an extremely specialized form of ethnography. It would no doubt surprise someone studying a college French course to be told that he was really an over-specialized anthropologist.[9]

In fact language study faces in two different directions. One leads to the whole culture which may be contained within the frame of reference of a single language. The other leads to the nature of language as a social and cultural phenomenon: it is this direction, needless to say, which concerns the anthropologist. Here there is so much work to be done that the study of language, particularly as part of a general theory of communication, is much more a subject in its own right, than a part, merely, of social anthropology.

SYMBOL, MYTH AND TOTEM

The true potential of the symbol is to communicate between two separate worlds. A good symbol has meanings at two different levels, the prosaic and the esoteric. The prosaic relates directly to ordinary day-to-day existence. It is therefore entirely language bound, and may be expressed, variously, in the language of any culture which recognizes the symbol.

Let us take two examples, the first a fleeting one from the present day, the second, an enduring one with its place in the whole history of the world. To show the narrowness of the prosaic meaning, it may be expressed, for each of the two examples, in unfamiliar languages:

1st symbol: 'Mettere un tigre nel motore'
2nd symbol: 'Loku ku umzimba wami, owa hlepulelwe nina'.

The reader who can understand neither of these languages will be immediately enlightened—and at the same time liable spontaneously to translate them into English—as soon as he is shown the right symbol for each of them. That for the first sentence is

: it is almost unnecessary to add that the English version is 'Put a tiger in your tank'.[10]

But consider this sentence a little more closely. First as to form: it is utterly prosaic, and makes no use whatever of any aesthetic power of the English language. Second as to linguistic content: inherently it lacks any meaningful referents. One is left asking, Which tiger? What tank? The tank of course, is the petrol tank of your car. It would not only be impossible to get a tiger into it, but completely useless. But, third, look at the context, which has two aspects. The first, again, is prosaic. The tiger symbol appears in advertisements for ESSO petrol, and in particular it is displayed at ESSO petrol stations. So the message is 'Use ESSO petrol in your car'. But why? This leads to the second aspect of the context, which consists of the whole inherited popular culture as it refers both to tigers and to cars—which, of course, is what ESSO's advertising agents were trading on from the beginning. The tiger is seen as a supremely powerful animal, and power is precisely what the motorist is looking for in his car. The symbolic message is that the act of pumping ESSO petrol into a car, transfers to the engine the quasi-mythical power of the tiger—as if the reader did not know this already.

But look now at the symbol which goes with the second foreign language sentence. (This is actually in Zulu—a language, incidentally, not so far used in ESSO advertisements.) This second symbol is

the familiar communion wafer of the catholic church. The words which go with it. 'This is my body, which is broken for you', are subject to precisely the same analysis as the words of the ESSO advertisement. At the prosaic level one is left asking, 'Whose body?' or, cynically perhaps, 'So what?' Now the actual identification of the consecrated host with the body of Christ and the sacramental theology of the Eucharist, are no part of this book. But the concern here is with one of the most condensed of all symbols. The New Testament is constantly concerned with the life-giving body, and its identification with bread, the essential food of life. It would be interesting to pursue the theme of the body as the common meeting point of theology and social anthropolgy.

As anthropologists however, we can only concern ourselves with the Eucharist in the context of any Christian culture. This leads from symbol to myth. The myth in the present case, is contained in the whole Christ event, not so much as it is recorded in the Bible, but more as it has been transmitted, in popular culture, throughout the history of the Church. (The anthropologist, unlike the theologian, cannot talk about the 'historical Jesus'.) The myth explains the symbol, and the symbol comprehends the myth.[11] The role of the myth is to furnish a sort of cultural starting point, a sort of enduring anchor for the culture: it is indeed significant how often in tribal cultures, the mythopoeic base remains constantly at the same distance in the past. (This is comparable, in physics, to the speed of light, which is always constant in relation to that of any moving object—as Einstein showed.) It is myth which creates the 'other' world, and symbol which then provides the means of communicating between that world and our own. This explains why those who control the 'symbols' in any society—who may be a 'priesthood'—hold so much power, and are so jealous of their prerogatives. Significantly, then, a society may restrict the knowledge and interpretation of certain myths and symbols to initiates into a particular group.

In such a case the rite of initiation is itself likely to be highly symbolic. A good example of this is the circumcision of adolescent boys

among the Ndembu of Zambia.[12] This is related to a three-fold colour symbolism of white, black and red. White, which is associated with the idea of making visible—or *kusolola*—is the key colour. But black, representing death and discontinuity, and red, symbolizing the uncleanness, play essential supporting roles. The uncircumcised boy lacks whiteness, and at the same time is characterized by the impurity of a woman at her menses, with the inevitable association of the *red* of her menstrual blood, or of his blood shed in the actual circumcision operation. This, in turn, reveals the actual glans of the penis, whose symbolic colour is white. The white symbolism is found also in the fact that the first of the new initiates sleeps on the leaves of the *mudi*, or 'milk' tree. These are then burnt to provide a *black* ash—or *mfunda*—which is used by the actual circumciser in closing each stage of the ceremony. He personifies the lion, the 'killer' of boys, at the end of every such stage. (Compare the use of the 'lion' in British advertising to associate by means of *shape*, a particular emotion with a particular commodity. See diagram on p. 109.) This is only one example of the ordering of the Ndembu universe in terms of the interrelationship of the three symbolic colours.

The mythopoeic base of Ndembu circumcision is rather ill-defined. There are a number of myths, but they have in common the original and accidental, circumcision of one particular boy by a blade of grass. This then became an example which others followed, with great benefit to themselves. And so the way was left open to develop all the symbolic accretions described above. These are significant for their high degree of abstraction. Red, white and black are almost universal conceptual categories, as are also some at least of the things they refer to—such as blood for red, milk for white, or ash for black.

Myth, also, is characterized by the comparative fewness of its themes, and the wide extent of their distribution. The familiar narratives of the book of Genesis, telling of the creation of man, or of his surviving a great flood, or of his dispersion over the face of the earth—to speak countless different tongues, all have their parallels in tribal mythologies. In myth the same story is told over and over again, with contradictions in detail which no historian would tolerate, but with the essential theme constantly upheld.[13] This makes myth highly translatable. It relates an existential fact, such as the diversity of language, to a narrative which explains it; it enables any society, culturally speaking, to define its boundaries.

Myth and symbol naturally lead on to primitive religion, which is the subject of Chapter 8. But nothing is said there of one particular institution—the *totem*. Now the history of totemism in anthropology is very confusing. Our own popular culture comprehends it, but only to treat it very unscientifically.

What then is a totem? Or better, what is it not? It is not necessarily an animal representation of a mythical object of worship or taboo. Totemism is not the basic primitive religion, which, indeed, has no one particular form.[14] Essentially a *totem* is no more than a symbol drawn from nature which may be identified, for certain purposes, with a particular group or individual. At the lowest level a name may have certain totemic properties—consider all the English people called 'Fox'.[15]

The role of totemism is essentially structural.[16] It serves to differentiate groups or individuals from each other in such a way as to determine the relationship between them in terms of that assumed between their respective totems. Thus in one Australian tribe there are two exogamous moieties, one with the eagle-hawk as its totem, the other with the crow. Here the totemic principle simply differentiates the two moieties. But implicit also is the fact that the eagle-hawk is a bird of prey, and the crow, a scavenger, which imports a complementary relationship based on the body of one animal eaten by them. This, in turn, may be elaborated mythopoeically in a way significant for the organization of the local society. In this way totemism becomes part of the same conceptual system as myth and symbol, and may equally have a part to play in the ritual life of the tribe. But totemism implies the combination of symbols in a significant way; it provides a sort of grammar of symbolism, although by no means the only one. It is structurally defective, in that it lacks depth: in Chomsky's terms it is not a generative grammar.[17] It is as incomplete as a language with a vocabulary consisting only of nouns would be—although it is worth noting that some totemic vocabularies are very large.

Since symbolic systems, such as totemism, of essentially limited range, always exist side by side with language, what function have they which they perform better than language? The answer is that the generality of language makes it needlessly over-elaborate, and unwieldy in its application in certain critical contexts. These are highly specific in institutional and ecological terms, and have a high level of interaction within themselves. This is implicit in the symbolic system developed for every such context, whether it is the totemism which relates to prescribed marriage systems in Australia,[18] or the road-signs which guide the motorist in the modern world.

A restricted symbolic system is also subject to political (or bureaucratic) manipulation and control, in a way which language never can be. (This is paradoxical, in so far as language is a creation of man.) A whole study could be made of symbolic innovations devised for use in political movements: this would reveal a sort of latter-day development of totemism. The study could be extended to the mythologies which such movements appeal to. This is just one example of the significance of anthropology for the present day: the institutions of the simple society are constantly to be found, only highly disguised, in our own.

WRITING AND PRINTING

Visual means of communication, of one sort or another, are to be found in every society. But in tribal societies their range is likely to be extremely narrow, and in no sense could they be said to be a counterpart of the spoken language. We have already looked at a number of visual signs and symbols, and it is clear that none of these are capable of being extended to cover the same field as the spoken word. Just think for a moment how you would express the above sentences using only international road-signs. The idea cannot begin to be taken seriously.

The real obstacle to the development of writing was that the intuitive way of representing a word, at least in primitive thought, was not to establish a visual correlate of the sounds comprised in the word, but to create a stylized picture of what the word meant. That is, the intuitive way to write the word 'house' was to draw something looking like a house, rather than to invent a visual code, conventionally accepted, which was apt to represent this, or indeed any other word of the local language in terms of how it sounded. Now by allowing pictographic writing to become more and more stylized (and therefore less obviously related, visually, to what it represents), it may be extended so as to express any possible sentence in the spoken language. This is exactly what is done by written Chinese.[19] At this stage, however, the relationship between the individual written character and its meaning becomes entirely esoteric, and therefore must quite simply be learnt by anyone wishing to use the written language. There is no short-cut from a knowledge of any spoken version of Chinese to understanding the written language, which has inevitably become almost infinitely complex— and at the same time essentially divorced from any form of speech. (This does have the advantage that two educated Chinese can write to each other, even though their speech would be mutually incomprehensible.)

The difficulty is that the physical properties of sound are not really comparable to those of light: in human terms, the ear is an essentially different organ to the eye, and what man can create with his vocal chords, in the realm of sound, is essentially different to what he creates with his hands in the realm of light. They are two different worlds, and writing could never develop beyond the pictograph until in some way, which had to be purely conventional, they were reconciled.

The first step towards this reconciliation—itself the most decisive cultural innovation in the history of man—is to be found in the merest handful of Semitic scripts of the second millennium B.C. For these abandoned the usual representation of ideas (after the manner of written Chinese) for the representation of sounds, by means of syllabaries, whereby every sign, conventionally, represented one particular spoken syllable. Once this step had been taken, the more analytic alphabetical system—which first evolved in ancient Greece —followed very quickly. An alphabet, suitably devised, is apt to provide a perfect visual and material correlative to any spoken language; the idea of the alphabet depends on a universal, but entirely abstract, property of speech, which is that in any language, no more than about forty different sounds—out of the almost unlimited number which the human speech mechanism can produce—are actually used. But the intuition that this property of speech might form the basis of a systematic visual representation of its content was for man an immense leap forward. The alphabet, perfectly developed in Greece nearly 3,000 years ago, is the classic case of cultural diffusion. All alphabets used today owe something to this single source. But the link between the written and the spoken word remain purely conventional. English could as well be written by using 'b' for 'a' and 'c' for 'b', and so on: we call this sort of thing a *code*, but forget that writing is itself a code. Indeed it is significant that Malay, for instance, is written both in Latin and Arabic characters: no doubt a Malay who normally uses Latin characters, thinks of the Arabic as comprising a sort of code, and vice versa. And now, for English, to make things easier for children, there is the initial teaching alphabet. This is no more than a new code, which happens to apply the alphabetical principle more systematically to the sounds actually found in spoken English.

So much for the inherent properties of writing: what interests anthropologists are its social consequences.[20] But at this stage the prospect becomes quite overwhelming, and the anthropologist, if he is not to write a critique of all that goes under the name of 'civilization', must surrender to the historian. The spoken word is carried away on the wind: the written word endures, and may be carried to the other end of the world, even to be read by generations yet unborn. So writing enables social organization and cultural diffusion of unprecedented scale and complexity. In some societies the control of this potent symbolism is retained by a narrow and exclusive class—often of priests. They may encourage the worship of sacred texts, sometimes called grapholatry—a practice epitomized by Tibetan Buddhism. To treat the written language as something arcane is essentially sterile—it is not surprising that this is more characteristic of non-alphabetical scripts.

The first general use of writing is in social control. Its appearance seems to be linked with the establishment of hierarchical societies, with masters and slaves. Most early writing consists of inventories, indentures catalogues, leases, laws and instructions—documents which reflect the power exercised by some men over other men and over their worldly possessions. Even in our own world a vast amount of written material is still of this kind: 'literature' is almost an epiphenomenon of literacy.

The social differentiation which writing enables has a cultural counterpart. Culture may be seen as an interacting set of communications, which in tribal societies are by the spoken word. Writing is an additional, rather than alternate means, of communication. Whereas the use of speech is acquired education in the home, literacy requires in practice the help of some external institution, which we recognize as the school. This is the most characteristic institution of any literate culture. In any society—with very few exceptions—those who can read and write, are those who have been to school. And the school is a corporate institution of a centralised hierarchical social system, such as the state.

In most 'literate' societies, literacy is in fact the property only of a schooled minority, which is closely related to the governing class—although its membership may not be precisely the same. Now communication by the written word is an individual and private matter: reading and writing are essentially solitary occupations. At the same time the corpus of written material, being nearly indestructible is so vast that any use of it must be highly selective. (This explains why the political control of literacy is so much concerned with prescribing which works are actually selected: this is the whole rationale of censorship.) The result is that the use of literacy, at least by the dominant cultural minority, is likely to be extremely individualistic. Here, as they say, 'Quot homines, tot sententiae'. This encourages a certain intellectual anarchy, but at the same time ensures a continual, and potentially creative interaction, between the different members of the educated minority. This is in complete contrast to the collective and homeostatic processes of any preliterate culture, which work by forgetting or transforming those parts of the oral tradition that cease to be necessary or relevant to the circumstances of the day.

Finally, what are the social consequences of printing? It overcomes what is otherwise the most serious drawback to the use of writing, that it is extremely laborious. Printing enables publication on an entirely different scale: far more works can be produced, in infinitely greater numbers for each one of them. In every dimension the scale is increased from the hundreds to the millions. Literacy can become *popular* in any society. The natural end of printing is essentially democratic. This does not mean a reversion to the classless society, at least in the sense of any tribal culture. Judged historic-ally printing has enabled the growth of bureaucracy as a distinctive kind of political, economic and social organization. The priesthood of bureaucracy is that part of it which controls all the mass of printed material which regulates our day-to-day life, of which, again, works of scholarship or literature are no more than a sort of sugar-coating. This priesthood is the faceless 'them' of authority contrasted to the 'us' of the people. The hard core of their literary output consists of inelegant forms which must be completed in triplicate, and are published by the million. One might wish that our bureaucracy, as that of ancient Akkadia, was still restricted to clay tablets. Files, not books, are the real hall-mark of contemporary literary output. They leave little scope for the 'structural amnesia' of oral tradition: at best (or at worst) they can get lost. Now the process which started with the hieroglyph and the pictogram has outreached the original concept of visual record and communication, and is being reduced to a code on a magnetic tape which only an electronic computer can interpret. Here we enter into the realm of languages, such as that of pure mathematics, which are inherently divorced from speech, and have their own autonomy. These are only within the province of cultural anthropology at a very esoteric level. Indeed one is half inclined to fear that one day a computer culture will reduce anthropology—which is to do with man in all his diversity—to being next to meaningless.

But to consider further the social consequences of such meta-languages as are used between computers would lead from social science to science-fiction, and would require as an author, a novelist rather than a scholar.[21] In the twenty-first century, no doubt, this particular subject will have been overtaken by history, and be part of contemporary sociology.

8

Gods and Spirits: Witches and Ancestors

THE COSMOS IN PRIMITIVE THOUGHT

In our own advanced society we see religion in a light quite different to that of any primitive people. To us religion is something set apart, which is directly concerned only with certain aspects of our existence. This concern is expressed in terms of doctrines, rituals and, to a lesser extent moral rules, whose social impact comes mainly from the free adherence to them of individual members of our society. We are almost encouraged to be selective and highly individualistic in our approach to religion. This means that our religions, viewed objectively, are essentially social movements whose success varies with the extent of their popular support.

This approach would be impossible for any primitive society. Primitive thought does not see religion as a distinct social or intellectual institution. To the primitive mind religion is an inseparable part of a whole world-view, which we may call a 'cosmology'. According to our ideas, we may certainly be able to identify something in primitive society which we may set aside and call 'religion': indeed there have been any number of anthropological studies of 'primitive religions'. But the distinctions upon which our understanding of religion depends, such as between the 'natural' and the 'supernatural', or the 'physical' and the 'metaphysical', have a quite different form in primitive thought.

Primitive religion is therefore part of the total culture of the society. The idea that one man could be a Methodist and another a Roman Catholic would be very difficult to grasp, except in terms which would completely distort the true nature of the distinction between them—at least as we see it. There is an essential unity about a primitive society, which its religion will express, just as there is about primitive culture. It could be said that where the social structure of a primitive people expresses the actual relationships between the living members of the society, the religious structure incorporates not only these persons, but also the spirits of the departed together with various other spirits, gods and powers, and so on, and it expresses the putative relationships which are believed to exist between all of them. This makes the social structure no more than the visible part of the religious or 'cosmological' structure. And since the 'cosmos' represents the totality of possible human experience and achievement, any part of the primitive material culture, as for instance its graphic arts, is certain to be 'religious'. An exhibition of Gothic art, such as was put on at the Louvre in Paris in 1967, makes the point admirably clear for medieval Europe, which represents in our history the end-point of our religious society.

Essentially, therefore, a study of primitive religion is a study of the different means which the culture of a primitive society may adopt to evoke a 'cosmos' of which that society, as it exists at any time, will be no more than the current picture on the cosmic television screen. In this way the vision of primitive man is extended beyond the circumstances of his day-to-day living. Primitive cosmology therefore gives to such circumstances a perspective which they would not have otherwise. This result seems to require in practice a sharp differentiation, affirmed particularly by the rituals of primitive society, between two different states, which the great French sociologist, Durkheim, labelled the 'sacred' and the 'profane', perhaps rather misleadingly.[1] They might better be called the 'abnormal' and the 'normal' and in any case they are not necessarily to be equated with, say, the 'supernatural' and the 'natural'. The idea is more that life—including what we would think of as the supernatural life—is generally 'normal', but that inevitably there are 'abnormal' phases, in which the order of things is reversed. These phases may occur at special seasons, such as the New Year, in which case they will affect the whole community, or at special periods in the life of a group, such as the 'initiation' of an age-set,[2] or at a special time in the life of an individual, such as pregnancy and childbirth.[3] The reversal of the normal order is expressed in a number of ways, some negative, such as the exclusion of the persons concerned from society, or the prohibition of certain foods—these are typical 'taboos'—and others positive, such as special rites and ceremonies, often directed by special officials—or 'priests'—which may articulate the theme of 'reversal' by prescribing behaviour—for instance, ritual 'homosexuality'—of a kind normally forbidden.[4] This polarization in primitive life is commonly explained by its mythology; indeed to Lévi-Strauss this is the fundamental theme of all folk-lore, which he sees as resolving, if in countless different modes, a basic conflict between nature and culture.[5] There is no need to accept the whole of Lévi-Strauss' analysis, but the idea of the 'normal' and the 'abnormal', and of their relationship to each other, is essential. The march of time, the cycle of the seasons, and the on-going process of the individual life, all combine to make certain that the 'normal' cannot be continuously preserved.[6] In many different circumstances the normal must be abandoned, but only to be restored again by the 'abnormal' procedures. This process is the essential dynamics of primitive religion, and, if grasped at its deepest level, it will provide the key to the understanding of many of the institutions of primitive society.

THE ENDS OF PRIMITIVE RELIGION

Man, everywhere, in his day to day life, is continually having to come to terms with nature. In the end everything which we need for our well-being derives from some natural product of the earth. The minerals which we exploit, or the crops which we cultivate, or the living creatures which we herd or hunt or trap, are none of them part of what man himself has created. Animal and plant life exists only at this natural level, although the natural forces which control it may be directed by man. But man, at every level, improves upon nature, essentially by means of his technology. Even the most primitive stone age man, who feeds himself by digging up roots, has a rudimentary technology which is essential for sustaining the life of his society.[7]

Now man, if he controls nature, nowhere overcomes it. We cannot, for instance, escape from our own natural mortality. Nor can we change the processes by which new life, and especially new human life, is created. We can use every modern method of agriculture, and yet we still cannot predict the harvest: we may understand the processes of meteorology, but we cannot control the weather. Now it is only humanity at a very advanced level which looks upon all these incidents of nature with a scientific eye. This gives to us, at one and the same time, both a certain arrogance and a certain humility. We are arrogant because we have discovered a systematic technique for unravelling the mysteries of nature, and directing them to our own ends. We are humble because we know, scientifically, our limitations: we know that natural processes, in the end, have their own authority, or better, perhaps, integrity.

This is not the world of primitive man. In his thinking the

forces which his limited technology cannot control are not for that reason beyond control. Quite the opposite: all forces operate because they are directed by some agency, which may be explicit in the technology, or implicit in the cosmology. Take the example of a crop planted for harvest. At one level this is a matter of technology. The ground has to be prepared, the seed planted, the crop harvested. But none of this is sufficient without the right co-ordination of natural forces. The seed must grow in the ground, the ear must ripen on the stalk, and all this requires rain and sunshine in due season. These matters are never left to chance, so it is part of primitive cosmology to control them. This is why the primitive cosmos is the realm of all kinds of beings and powers: they are an essential part of man's interaction with nature, which is critical to his survival. So primitive religion is a matter of defining, identifying, influencing and controlling these beings and powers. This provides the rationale of all primitive ritual, which may be said to consist of those actions of primitive man whose meaning and intent are extrinsic to their content: that is, the end intended from a ritual act is not scientifically deducible from the act itself, but is rather a given part of the local culture.

Religion, in this sense, operates at many different levels. An individual, going out to hunt alone, will first follow a ritual designed to encourage an abundance of game. A man, with a new wife, will by the appropriate ritual ensure that she conceives a child. A sick man will use ritual to diagnose and cure his sickness.

Religion plays an equally important part in the life of the group, or of the whole society. Religious thought and action provide the proper response to every disaster—drought, famine, plague[8] and so on—which may come upon a people. Its most significant role, perhaps, relates to the annual cycle of seasons, so that in every new year there will be enough food for the people. This is why the first fruits of the harvest are so often set aside as a religious offering. This explains also why certain roles are specifically associated with the power to bring rain: examples are the Alur chiefs[9] or the Dinka spear-masters,[10] or, most particularly, the rain-queen of the Lovedu of the Transvaal, whose health is regarded as essential to an abundant rainfall.[11] The seasonal ceremonies tend to bring the people together, thereby affirming the important social dimension of religion, in which the whole structure of the local society may be reflected by the allocation of different religious offices. The function of primitive religion is largely to give an idealized picture of society, which may provide a model for regulating its affairs.

Religion plays an extremely important part in the great crises of life—birth, adolescence, marriage, pregnancy and death. On all such occasions there must be special rites, ensuring that the individual passes through the crisis, so as to achieve the right social status after it. These special rites are known as *rites de passage*, a name given to them by the French anthropologist, Arnold van Gennep.

Now any *rite de passage* has three stages, separation from the previous state, transition and incorporation into the new state.[12] In the Christian theology of Augustine of Hippo, one may consider the birth of a new child as requiring first its reparation from its mother's womb, and at the end its incorporation, by baptism, into the Church, with an abnormal period of transition in between, in which, if the child dies, its soul can go only to limbo. But much more critical in any primitive society are the rites to be performed at death, which ensure that the deceased achieves whatever form is conceived as appropriate for his continued non-worldly existence. For primitive man mortuary customs are likely to have an almost sacramental importance, of a kind which Christianity allows only to baptism.[13]

One must be more precise about what mortuary customs are meant to achieve. The dead man, often according to what he has been in his earthly life, is seen as destined for a special role beyond the grave. For example, in a society with ancestor worship, such as that of the Tallensi, the member of the senior generation in a family who dies leaving descendants of his own lineage should qualify automatically as an 'ancestor', provided the right mortuary customs, ending with the prescribed rite of incorporation, are observed.[14] (Failure to observe them would leave the dead man as a sort of unhappy discarnate spirit, who would perpetually trouble his surviving descendants: this is unthinkable.) But once the final rite is performed, the 'ancestor' has all the power, with the con-comitant need to be worshipped, which local tradition assigns to ancestors.

In another society the effect of the mortuary customs may be to incorporate the deceased in the community of a paradisal state, such as the Trobriand islanders conceive as existing on the island of Tuma, whence the departed returned once a year to their villages, to dance—invisibly, it need hardly be said—in the Milamila festival. This has little to do with ancestor worship of the Tallensi type. The Trobrianders also believe that in the end one returns from

Tuma to be reincarnated in a new life:[15] the Fon of Dahomey couple such a belief with ancestor worship, and in particular they see their kings always as reincarnating other kings—endowed with the right personalities—of the past.[16]

The rites of adolescence often best illustrate the primitive cosmology. They have the advantage—to the anthropologist—that the subject may be observed at every stage, which is plainly impossible for the rites surrounding birth and death. (This, a scientific distinction, would mean little in primitive thought). Primitive society differentiates the initiated adult very sharply from the uninitiated child. The period of transition, and the rites associated with it, may be very protracted, and the occasion of all kinds of abnormal behaviour. They will often include an operation, such as circumcision, which will permanently and visibly distinguish the initiate.[17]

Primitive religion, then, is an aspect of culture whose function it is to enable man to come to terms with inexorable natural forces, and most particularly those connected with the on-going cycle of birth and death. But cosmology and culture are not terms of primitive thought: what primitive man sees is the universe going on day after day under the impact of forces—both natural and supernatural as we would see them—which the right human actions will control. And if these actions fail, as often they do, the failure is not scientific, but moral, and morality is part of culture.[18]

THE STRUCTURE OF THE PRIMITIVE COSMOS

In the religious thinking of primitive man the cosmos exists at different levels of progressively greater abstraction. The end-point at the highest level may be one *high god*, who may be seen as endowed with moral attributes of supposedly universal application. But the exclusive rule of such a god is difficult, if not impossible, for man to sustain in society, as witness the trouble which the ancient Hebrews constantly had with idolatry.[19] What is needed is a much lower level of cosmic existence, which may be conceived according to a model which relates directly—and therefore intelligibly—to the actual world. At this level the model—which to our way of thinking will be conceptual or imaginary—will almost inevitably reflect the most important institutions of the primitive society.

The model will have a number of component parts structurally related to each other, in such a way as to idealize, and yet, at the same time, regulate the actual social organism. In psychological terms the model is a projection of the society, and it is one which enables the society to come to terms with itself. The interaction of the different components of the model will sometimes reflect actual social conflicts: more often the function of the model, as observed by an outsider, is to encourage stability in the society.

To dispel the air of mystery which may now prevail, one or two examples must be given of what it all adds up to. The first will be of the spirit world of the Kalabari, a people of Southern Nigeria who live in relatively isolated villages and traditionally support themselves by fishing in the creeks of the Niger delta.[20] Here three different aspects of life are important: the first is the lineage into which one is born, the second, the village of which one is a resident, and the third, the success of one's fishing. Now there is a particular spirit which controls every individual person, plant, animal or thing, but there are in addition three categories of free spirits which correspond to the three 'aspects' mentioned above. These are the *duen*, or departed ancestors, the *am'oru*, or mythical village heroes, and the *owuamapu*, or water-people. Now in Kalabari religion these three groups will interact, and indeed sometimes conflict, just as the different aspects which they represent do in everyday life. Each one of the three categories will have its own autonomy, but may none the less be induced to act in some desired manner by the right ritual approach. So in a matter affecting the welfare of a lineage, a sacrifice will be made at the ancestor shrine: indeed there will be a recognized round of sacrifices which, hopefully, will keep the 'ancestors' happy at all times. Indeed, if some misfortune of the lineage makes it clear that the ancestors are displeased, this will not be attributed to their own caprice, but to some failure in the ritual approach made to them.

Turning now to the water-people, some of their activities may be represented by masked dances performed by a special society known as *Ekine*. The religious and social values represented by the Ekine masquerades are somewhat ambiguous, but this is not the point: the dances are a means whereby an unreal dimension of the cosmos is visibly expressed. The masks are important, first for concealing the identity of the actors (almost sure to be known personally to the spectators), and second because they enable the play to achieve a measure of abstraction and permanence, which would otherwise be quite impossible. A mask represents no particular human being, and if well-made, it may last to be worn by several generations of players.

Among the Kono of Guinea[21] it is the masks which personify and enforce the moral code; they order the *rites de passage*, particularly of initiation; they protect, guide and punish the individual. Here there are special masks for each different function, and although the persons who wear them belong each to a prescribed lineage, and have to be ritually installed, this, again, is not the point. Any one mask is only worn for its own special occasions, when its effectiveness depends on its religious attributes much more than on the personality of the individual who wears it. Indeed the prescribed ritual goes far to efface his individuality. He is sewn into a special garment, so that even his hands are invisible, and he must not leave visible footprints when he walks. The role of the mask is ascribed to it by tradition, and authenticated in mythology. Here their role, although not involving dancing, is much more important than with the Kalabari. But again the mask has a life of its own, as is shown by the sacrifice which has to be made when a new mask replaces one which is worn out—for the essence of sacrifice is to transfer, symbolically, the life of the victim to another person.

At this lowest non-worldly level of the cosmos, one may abstract from different societies a sort of scale of different beings who control it. The Kalabari village heroes existed only in mythology, the lineage ancestors once actually lived, but now departed, only exist to affect the lives of those still living, the wearers of the Kono masks actually live, but the masks have an independent existence; all of them play a part in the actual day to day life of the community. Another step down the scale leads to witchcraft, which superimposes a world of witches—who are actually living people—upon the actual visible world of everyday life. Taking the case of the Azande[22] (of the Sudan-Zaire border region) these people see almost every misfortune as being sent by a witch. And the witches are ordinary people, but the world which they inhabit, as witches, is unreal, and hardly ever does any individual learn that he is himself thought to be a witch. His victims recognize him as such, generally as a result of consulting an oracle. But it is almost inherent in the action taken against him (which will be based on magic), that he never gets to know of it. To take an extreme case, suppose that X dies, then his family will learn from the oracle that the death was caused by, say, the member of a certain lineage, against which magic will be directed. Then, after a few months, Y, a member of that lineage, may happen to die, and the family of X will assume that their magic has avenged X's death. Y's family, of course, will think quite differently, and they, by the same process, will no doubt pin everything on Z, a member of yet a third lineage, and so on. Here Y is the critical case, because he is both a witch, and bewitched. Of course there is conflict in the Zande system, but their society has the right institutions for controlling it. At the same time Zande witchcraft implies a very definite *Weltanschauung*, common to all the Azande—almost every significant happening in daily life is comprehended within this world-view. This explains why Zande religion beyond the realm of witchcraft is rather ill-defined. In a sense the Azande have no 'theology': their witchcraft suffices for all 'religious' purposes.

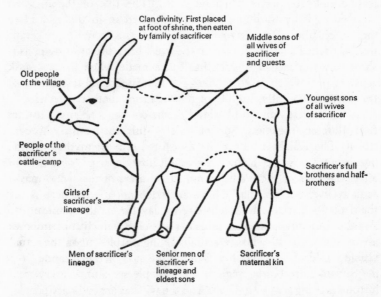

The Dinka treat their cattle as ideally representing and controlling human relations:[23] they are almost equivalent to the masks of the Kono or the ancestors of the Tallensi. The interaction between men and cattle may be made explicitly on the occasion of a sacrifice, for the carcass is then divided according to the diagram above, in which the part to be given to the clan divinity should be particularly noted.

The Dinka sacrifice is significant as illustrating one means of achieving the interaction between society and the lowest level of the cosmos, which is plainly essential if the whole cosmic structure is to mean anything at all. Much more could be said about the essential symbolism, whereby this interaction is expressed, and established in the tradition of different societies, as also about the ritual means of achieving it. But now one must ascend to the higher levels of the cosmos, and more particularly to the great world religions.

JUDGEMENT AND THE UNIVERSAL GOD

If to us the Kono masks, the Tallensi ancestors, the Zande witches or the Dinka cattle seem each to inhabit a realm of incredible complexity, this is only because the lowest level of the primitive cosmos must relate directly to the world of the local society, which is even more complex. Otherwise it would not provide in sufficient measure the necessary agencies for controlling and directing the day to day activities of the people. In our own world we find all the complexity of the primitive cosmos in the multiform institutions of law, science and bureaucracy: where our 'number' is recorded in a file in the income tax office—or perhaps, today, on the odd millimetre of magnetic tape—that of the average Dinka may be found in the appropriate part of a sacrificial ox. The point is that in either case— the primitive or advanced—this lowest level of the cosmos is no more than the first degree of abstraction from the social structure of the actual world of the living. In fact the abstract is much simpler than the reality from which it derives: even a complicated cosmos such as that of the Kalabari is much simpler than their actual society.

Primitive man, in any case does not stop at this first level of the cosmos he may ascend by a succession of further abstractions, to yet higher levels, ending with one high god. An example is the Dinka 'Nhialic', who is seen as refracted in every experience of the people.[24] And just as one may see the lowest level of the cosmos as being no more than the first degree of abstraction from social reality, so also it may be seen—and this is how the Dinka would see it—as a particularized manifestation of the experience of divinity. It depends on whether one starts with man or God. And different sorts of events may be assigned to different levels of the cosmos: thus the Lugbara, of northern Uganda, see sickness as generally caused by the ancestors, whereas death is caused by the act of their one high god.[25]

The religious life of primitive society may concentrate more on the least abstract, and therefore most complex level of the cosmos, simply because this, of its nature, interacts more immediately with day to day life. On the other hand, at this level, the cosmology is inherently restricted, whether in its historical or geological dimension. This is reflected in the fact that most primitive peoples do not begin to claim that their religion has anything to do with anyone but themselves. We would, for instance, find it next to impossible to adopt the Dinka cattle cosmology to the circumstances of our modern industrial state, simply because cattle in no way play a comparable part in our lives—not even for those of us who are dairy farmers. But we could take over *Nhialic* quite easily, except that in a rather trad way we would probably prefer to call him God.

We can now consider the key to success of the three great world religions: Hindu-Buddhism, Judaeo-Christianity and Islam—noting perhaps that even they tend to carve up the world into three great missionary areas. The Judaeo-Christian tradition is the best example for us, because it is the most familiar. Its universal appeal is very ancient, and it derives from the fact that at a very early stage, historically, Israel specifically repudiated every level of any possible cosmology beneath that of its one God, Yahweh, the Lord of all creation. This is the whole point to the commandments given to Moses on Mount Sinai, of which the first three, against polytheism, idolatry and blasphemy are religiously much the most significant. These would eliminate the Kalabari ancestors, heroes and water people, at the same time assuring the possibility of a world-wide appeal, which, historically, came only to be realized with the founding of the Christian church. But as the Jews have always found, if you have but one God, with no refractions of him at any lower level, he becomes impossibly remote. The 'hidden God' is a constant theme of Judaeo-Christianity, and it is really no part of a work on anthropology to explain how the situation was resolved by the Christ-event—although the universal potential of the Christian sacraments of baptism and communion is extremely significant.[26]

Now the Judaeo-Christian God—as any other God—has got to rule. Otherwise he would be a nonentity. Judged historically, an important, if variable, aspect of the way he rules—in the sense of controlling and directing and intervening in human life—is that he calls for obedience to a universal and unchanging code of law.

This in practice requires the use of writing, which has been indispensable for all the world religions,[27] and ensures that they forget nothing—which would very soon clog the machinery of ancestor worship. Judgement is inherent in the enforcement of a legal code, and the theme of judgement is most prominent in the world religions. True, primitive man may see an element of judgement in the failure of some ritual to achieve its end, but this is not on the cosmic scale of Judaeism or Christianity. Inevitably in Christianity,

Buddhism or Islam, the idea of judgement focuses upon the individual, and determines his destiny in another world. (In this world the unjust often do rather well for themselves.) The remote hidden God of Christianity or Islam, can only pronounce one sentence in judgement, which explains the terror of one like Martin Luther when he felt himself in the presence of God.[28] Buddhism, with no one God, mitigates its judgement of the dead by providing for everyone an endless cycle of earthly reincarnation.[29]

In practice the world religions have always required a cosmic structure to fill the space between their high god and their faithful adherents. This explains the incredible prolixity of the law in Rabbinic Judaeism (which is comparable to that of Christian or Buddhist monasticism) and even more the complex realm of saints, guardian angels, souls in purgatory and so on, which characterizes the cosmos of the Catholic church.[30] Protestantistism did away with all this, but at the cost, not only of eliminating many traditional religious institutions, but also of ushering in a new world of capitalism, bureaucracy and scientific technology. This is the cosmos which we all must come to terms with: its lowest level is the computer-complex which is coming to number the hairs on the heads of every one of us, and which may yet, with its esoteric symbolism of electronic circuitry, attain that universality which always eluded the Dinka cattle. It analyses all our problems in endless and minute detail: it solves none of them. It has carried man to the moon, but the danger is that it will separate him irreversibly, from the good earth whence he came. Perhaps we should return to to the Dinka, and call our God 'Nhialic' after all.

THE END OF THE WORLD

The general picture of religion in modern society is that it is a force for resolving conflicts, maintaining the stability of social structures, and bringing man to terms with his mortality. This is the sort of way in which Marx looked upon the established religions of his day, although according to his sense of the class struggle, religion achieved its results by deceiving the proletariat into accepting an essentially false view of society, which would conceal the true nature of their common hardship and oppression. Religion, in this light, is essentially homeostatic: it ensures that the rich stay rich, and the poor stay poor. It is not for nothing that the Anglican Church of the nineteenth century has been described as the 'conservative party at prayer'.

All this presupposes a society divided into classes, and more particularly according to the possession of accumulated and inherited wealth. The classic primitive societies—the Dinka, the Kalabari, and so on—were never of this kind. But what happens when such a society comes into contact with another, much more advanced, such as that of a modern colonial power? There then comes a stage when the local society has had to change its institutions at the very deepest level in order to adjust to foreign colonial administration. At this stage new types of religion appear: they tend to be millenarian, which means that they predict the end of the world within the lifetime of some at least of their adherents. Very often the message of approaching doom originates with a local 'prophet' or 'messiah'. Now religion of this kind is essentially dynamic: the world can only end once. Its focus, far from being on the preservation of the institutions of society, is on their destruction.[31]

How does this come about? This question is best answered by an actual example of such a religion, the so-called cargo cults of Melanesia and New Guinea.[32] Here the primitive local people noted two particular things about the Europeans who came to occupy and rule their territory. The first was that they had far greater material wealth than had ever been seen before. The second was they had quite new and unfamiliar religions. Now in the thinking of the natives the first could only have followed from the second: they could not have begun to understand that the wealth of the Europeans was primarily the result of a much more sophisticated technology and economy with a very long history behind it. The answer could only be that the European had found means of supplicating unseen cosmic powers which brought an immeasurably greater response than anything the natives had ever had from essentially the same source. Significantly one result of Christian mission was for the different personalities of the Bible, from Adam and Eve to Jesus, to be incorporated into the local cosmology, with their cosmic roles being transformed in the process.

The natives then expected the missionaries to teach them the religious secrets of the Europeans, and when this inevitably failed to happen, and there was no wealth forthcoming on the European scale, the missions were often completely discredited. It made sense to the natives that the missionaries should not divulge the secrets: after all, they too were Europeans, and often relied on the colonial power to protect them.

Native society was therefore more than ready for any prophet who discovered the secret. Of course no-one ever appreciated the actual truth of the matter, which was that the wealth of the colonists had little to do with the religions of their missionary compatriots. A successful prophet had therefore to represent the secret in esoteric terms, and devise a ritual to supplicate the gods to overturn the actual social order, so that the local people took over all the power and wealth of the Europeans. Now the general idea of 'cargo' was that all this would be brought, from across the seas, by boat or aeroplane, in indestructible and inexhaustible supply. For this result one needed only to adopt the prophet's cult. Sometimes it would be the mythical ancestors of the people who would bring the cargo, at the same time destroying the European colonists. It followed from the nature of the cult that crops need no longer be cultivated, nor animals husbanded: instead a quay or a landing-strip might be built to receive the cargo. This is an all-or-nothing throw of the cosmic dice: of course every cargo cult must fail, but this does not prevent another taking its place. A cargo cult sees the whole life of the people as one great *rite de transition*: at the end of the day the holy remnant who have followed the Messiah will come into paradise. But the social dimension of cargo is an irreconcilable conflict between two different cultures, neither of which can accept the other on its own terms. Cargoism is a typical product of the friction which must then result. It is the absolute reverse of what is needed from a cosmology: but history reveals movements of this kind as common in conditions of rapid and drastic social and political change.

Millenarian movements, of which cargo cults are by no means the only example, are characteristic of under-privileged groups, who according to the organization of society imposed upon them, see no legtimate way of coming to terms with it. The basis of a millenarian cult is the overthrow of the existing order, generally within the lifetime of the majority of the cult's adherents. This has decisive political and moral consequences. Politically collaboration with the existing order becomes betrayal or apostasy, whereas the highest virtue lies in undermining it. (This, in a way, is paradoxical, since the eventual overthrow will be by means of some divine intervention, but the point is seldom taken by the millenarians themselves.) Morally, there can be a complete reverse of values, simply because most social values are established by tradition—and the cult of its nature supersedes tradition—and presupposes also that the existing order must be annihilated. Families can be abandoned, property destroyed, and crops left unsown.

Occasionally a millenarian movement achieves political success, but it will almost always have forfeited its original character before it does so. The only possible consequence of success is complete transformation, often into a form of government essentially similar to the one overthrown. Much more often, millenarian movements come and go, reflecting the essential unrest of an oppressed minority, often today a racial minority. The appeal, the organization, the supernatural content, remain the same, since they are the product of the same combination of circumstances. Such movements are the symptom of a divided society: they can be seldom counteracted by argument, largely because they arise among groups which have no real communication with the dominant classes in society. The tragedy is that it is the members themselves who suffer in the end from the failure of the promised millenium. To their oppressor, their movements are no more than an escape from reality, sometimes destructive, occasionally innocuous. Certainly, if the present day organization of society continues, and the interests of minorities are still not sufficiently regarded, millenarian movements, in all their variety, will be with us for a long time to come.

9
Conclusion

This book is entirely a product of that one per cent of man's historical span in which he has broken free from a way of life which was quite adequate for his survival over more than a million years. This might suggest that the whole balance of this book is wrong: it describes hardly at all the life and society and culture of the primitive hunters and gatherers. Yet this century, which has seen the first man on the moon, may well see the disappearance of the last man to follow this way of life, which was once the lot of all our ancestors. At the same time such a book as this one could only be a product of the culture and scientific outlook of the twentieth century.

Man broke out of his old stone age culture by discovering the cultivation of land, the herding of animals, the firing of clay, the spinning and weaving of natural fibres—accomplishments possessed by almost all the people mentioned in this book. We cannot tell how these discoveries were originally made. The homeostatic processes of primitive cultures discourage innovation, but in those first 2,000,000 odd years there was time enough for chance to produce the right technological break-through. It occurred first perhaps 13,000 years ago. Its result, at the end of the day, was to lead to societies of unprecedented complexity, which could exploit the natural resources of the world so as to create material wealth on an unprecedented scale. These developments went hand in hand with a growth in population so rapid that for all the million or more years of the human era, an overwhelming majority of all the men who have ever lived have been members of such complex modern societies, rather than hunters and gatherers. It could well be argued that if such primitive populations are still to be studied, it is only so as to provide the most complete possible record of them, to be available in the centuries to come, when they will be totally extinct. This is a rarefied academic motive for study and research, and seems somewhat unrealistic when it is the whole *genus* man that we are concerned with. Even an anthropologist, with a pure academic and scientific approach to his subject, would have to acknowledge its political dimensions. These concern not only the political institutions of the populations studied, but also the political context in which such study is carried on. Indeed the two can well be related to each other.

A hundred years ago there were two different kinds of motive for the systematic study of primitive peoples; the first was concerned with the political interests of European imperialism. The new colonies established in Africa and Asia presented the problem of working out suitable forms of administration and government for primitive peoples quite outside the domain of any European culture. This created the need for an applied anthropology, and it is not surprising that the earliest studies were focused on the overseas territories of the great nineteenth-century colonial powers. The second motive for anthropological study was also political, but in a quite different sort of way. The nineteenth century was a period when independent secular movements arose to question all kinds of traditional institutions, particularly those of religion and government. Primitive cultures often provided—or at least were thought to provide—counter-examples of such institutions, which could be used to discredit the claims of the traditional European establishments.

The best work came to be done when anthropologists broke free from the prejudices inherent in either of these two types of motivation. The end of the first, and essentially restricted, period of development may be associated with the name of Frazer:[1] the beginning of the second, and essentially creative period, with that of Malinowski.[2] The Malinowski period covers more than a generation of first-class scholars, many of whose works are cited in the present study. But students of anthropology are once again questioning the fundamental motivation of their subject. Malinowski can no longer be seen as our contemporary. The day of the tribal society is nearly over, and the social systems which must now be studied are those of complex societies, integrated into the world economy.

Tradition is strong in anthropology, as in any sub-culture; indeed anthoropology explains just why it is so strong. So this is a book which started in the Malinowski tradition, which still provides the fundamental methods and concepts of the subject. Yet almost every, chapter ends by a consideration of developments, and institutions, which go beyond this tradition. The anthropologist today is continually having to come to terms with politically loaded concepts, such as poverty, minorities, alienation, subversion, and he can well be uncertain about what they mean. Scientific method is largely based on noting differences, and using them as a basis of comparison. Why is it that the poor of Mexico City, as studied by Lewis,[3] can be characterized as a poor alienated and possibly subversive minority, when the Nuer, as studied by Evans-Pritchard,[4] cannot be so. Is not the answer that the poor of Mexico City are a part of our world, in a way in which the Nuer are not? If so, does this mean that we have a political commitment to them, which we never had to Evans-Pritchard's Nuer? The Nuer, as Evans-Pritchard saw them, were precisely as they were because they were not involved in our world: Lewis' Mexican poor are as they are, precisely because they are so involved.

This point has been well-made by Firth, though from an essentially conservative stand-point:

> Social anthropology faces a special problem. Unlike most of the other sciences, its most-prized raw material is evaporating. The people themselves, of course, for the most part are not disappearing. But they have been altering their way of life radically, especially in those aspects which were the special province of the social anthropologist to study.[5]

The answer may well be that the 'most-prized raw material' is not only evaporating, but was in any case becoming worked-out by the anthropologists. Some had already begun to suspect that however many more Tallensi's and Tikopia's might be studied, few new insights would come to the fore. At the same time every new anthropologist could be so preoccupied with finding his own exclusive tribal culture, that he would have little time to assimilate the work already completed.

Anthropology is more and more concerned with the study of partial and incomplete social systems, each subject to a continuous interaction with the world outside. It is the fact of such interaction which gives meaning to the concepts of poverty, minority, alienation and subversion, mentioned above. A great deal of work, both practical and theoretical, has yet to be done here simply in definition and analysis. The complexity of any modern society makes certain that there will be scope for almost unlimited future research. Moreover since one party to the critical interaction is a social system of which the researcher is himself a member, he has, in any terms, a moral responsibility quite different from that of the traditional anthropologist. This is the more so since the interaction is never between groups of equal power: the researcher, almost inevitably, is a member of the dominant group (whatever his personal sympathies may be), while the subordinate group is generally the focus of his research. That is, he can influence the interaction, as well as study it—indeed, more than this, his motive for study may well be so that he can the more effectively make his influence felt. This will accentuate the political involvement of the anthropologist, but if anthropology is to maintain its standing as a science, the political role of the student must always be subordinate to the academic.

Politics is largely a matter of following one alternative line of action against another. The principles for deciding which line to choose tend to be stated in the most general terms, which purport to be applicable to any local situation. Commonly enough political activists in the third world tend to state local political issues in the cosmic terms of Marxism or capitalism, when by tradition the local population has always thought, politically, in a quite different frame of reference. Generally speaking the main issue confronting the typical subordinate minority in the third world concerns the degree to which it should maintain its traditional institutions, rather than adapt and integrate them into those of the wider society.[6] For many such minorities, particularly those in the large city, this is scarcely an open question: a revolutionary reordering of the total society of which they are a part seems often to be the only way of redressing their grievances, although here one should be very careful about assessing the economic and political potential of such a revolution. It is too often the experience of the third world—and not only the third world—that something close to the old order always succeeds in re-establishing itself. The names are different: the essential political and economic structure is the same.

In the new third-world context anthropology seems destined for a confused and insecure role: what distinguishes it from development studies, political science, human geography, demography, and so on? There is no perfect answer to this question, but it may well be said that the role of anthropology is to serve all these other sciences, which it does by working out the most fundamental concepts, by ranging widely over every kind of human population, by considering every institution and belief on its own merits, and finally by having a most profound respect for man's ability—at every level—to transform his environment, to refine his culture, and to organize his society. Man is at one and the same time a uniquely gifted, and a uniquely handicapped species. The study of how he applies his gifts so as to overcome his handicaps, *that* is what anthropology is about.

NOTES

CHAPTER 1

1. This point is made very emphatically in Leach 1961, p. 1.
2. Firth 1936 is the basic study.
3. In economic anthropology, the approach of Firth 1939, which applies the concepts developed for studies of the modern world, should be contrasted with that of Bohannan and Bohannan 1968, which develops the concepts of the particular primitive societies studied.
4. See Devore and Washburn 1968, p. 96.
5. Rivers 1906.
6. Lévi-Strauss 1956 contains a general survey of the author's Brazilian research.
7. These themes are particularly developed in Chapter 4.
8. See the discussion of table manners in Lévi-Strauss 1967, and of the distinction between cooked and raw food in Lévi-Strauss 1964. The question of what the anthropologist takes for granted is discussed in Gluckman's "The Limits of Naieveté in Social Anthropology".
9. This particular myth is so widespread that there is no question of its having spread by diffusion from one particular source. It has its origins everywhere in oral tradition—for which see Vansina 1961.
10. The use of different animal species to classify human groups is an important subject in Lévi-Strauss 1969.
11. See Lienhardt 1961.
12. See Firth 1936.
13. Evans-Pritchard 1940, Chapter 5, describes a classic example of such sub-division.
14. This term originates in Durkheim 1933, Chapter 2. See also Chapter 5, below.
15. See Durkheim 1933, Chapter 3.
16. This term was originally proposed by Prof. Max Gluckman, of Manchester University. 'Tribal' is often used in much the same sense.
17. See Chapter 4.
18. See Lienhardt 1961.
19. See Chapter 5.
20. The distinction between status and contract is first made in Maine 1861.
21. This fascinating society—in which all members of the female sex (of *whatever age*) are always married—is described in Hart and Pelling 1959.
22. See Firth 1936.
23. See Turnbull 1965.
24. The Tallensi of Northern Ghana are an interesting case here, for

the population is divided into two groups, one seen as autochthonous, and the other as of immigrant stock: Fortes 1940, pp. 244–7.

25. Bohannan, L. 1958, p. 35 (in 1970 paperback edition).

26. See the entry under 'Ussher' in the Oxford Dictionary of the Christian Church.

CHAPTER 2

1. Genesis 3:16.

2. Genesis 3:19.

3. This analysis follows that of the introduction to Goody 1958.

4. These crises, and their associated ritual, are described in Van Gennep 1960, a classic anthropological study.

5. An example of the associated ritual and symbolism is given for the Ndembu of Zambia on p. 109.

6. Malinowski 1932b, pp. 140–5. The male sexual organs did however have a sort of auxiliary role.

7. E.g. the Mountain Arapesh of New Guinea: see Mead 1935, Chapter III.

8. This is the Trobriand belief: Malinowski 1932b, pp. 145–52.

9. This may seem now a rather conservative view.

10. Notes and Queries in Anthropology 1951, cited in Gough 1968, p. 49.

11. Evans-Pritchard 1951, pp. 108–9.

12. Gough 1968 describes the traditional institutions of Nayar marriage.

13. See Fox 1967, pp. 184–95.

14. This is the central them of Lévi-Strauss 1969a. See particularly the last chapter.

15. Evans-Pritchard 1951, pp. 74–99 gives but one of many examples of this. See also p. 23 below.

16. Radcliffe-Brown and Forde 1950, preface.

17. Lee and Devore 1968 contains an excellent comprehensive survey of hunters and gatherers.

18. See Lee 1968.

19. See Turnbull 1965.

20. See Smith 1956.

21. See Radcliffe-Brown and Forde 1950, p. 8 and Fox 1967, p. 187.

22. See Fox 1967, Chapter 6.

23. See Diagram 2A.

24. See Fox 1967, Chapter 4.

25. Bohannan, L. 1958, pp. 40–2.

26. In just the same way the promotion of new companies does not affect the practical operation (or advantages) of corporation law: see Radcliffe-Brown and Forde 1950, p. 43.

27. Ibid, pp. 47–54. See also p. 59 below.

28. See Evans-Pritchard 1940, Chapter V.

29. This is illustrated by Diagram 2B.

30. See Malinowski 1935, Vol. I, Chapter VI, Section 2.

31. See Douglas 1969, and Diagram 2C.

CHAPTER 3

1. Durkheim 1915 develops an extensive theory of religious life on the basis of these meetings. See p. 117 below.

2. Leach 1954.

3. Page 22.

4. See Evans-Pritchard 1940, pp. 152–8.

5. Based upon the diagram in Evans-Pritchard 1940, p. 144.

6. See Yablonski 1967.

7. See Wilson 1951. The Nyakyusa are by no means the only African tribe in which age-sets play a part in the political organization.

8. Bohannan, L. 1958, pp. 33–6.

9. Bohannan and Bohannan 1968 contains a complete description of the Tiv market systems.

10. Fortes 1940.

11. Evans-Pritchard 1940, Chapters IV and V.

12. Newcomer 1972 argues that the Nuer are in fact of Dinka origin.

13. See Evans-Pritchard 1962, Chapter 4: 'The divine kingship of the Shilluk of the Nilotic Sudan.'

14. See Southall 1956.

15. See Oberg 1940.

16. See Maquet 1954.

17. See Richards 1940.

18. See Mair 1962.

19. See Oberg 1940, p. 132.

20. Frazer 1922.

21. See Oberg 1940, pp. 157–61.

22. Mair 1962.

23. The problems of bureaucracy in a third world context is the subject of Fallers 1956, which is about the Busoga of Uganda. Bendix 1966 is a general study of Max Weber.

24. Bendix 1966, p. 424.

25. See Chapter 7 below.

26. See Chapter 6 below.

27. See Marx 1844.

28. Almost every anthropological field-worker must come across cases of corruption: it is difficult to report them in publications, for fear of jeopardizing contacts made in the course of research. But see Blok 1969 for a case where the unofficial system has almost taken over from the unofficial local bureaucracy.

29. For an analysis along these lines, see Boissevain 1968.

30. See Yablonski 1967.

CHAPTER 4

1. The first part of this chapter is largely based on ideas derived from Harris, D. R. 1969, pp. 4–7, and Geertz 1970, Chapter 1.

2. A notable example of this in a generalized eco-system is the

construction of the Kariba dam, across the Zambesi, between Rhodesia and Zambia, in the course of the 1960s.

3. An excellent early discussion of primitive diet is contained in Richards 1939, pp. 1–9.

4. Lee 1968, p. 33.

5. Woodburn 1968, p. 53.

6. Barnicot 1969, p. 526.

7. Harris, D. R. 1969, p. 6.

8. Lee 1968, p. 31.

9. Lee and Devore 1968, p. 3.

10. Balikci 1968.

11. Turnbull 1965. The present analysis is not meant to suggest that human kind necessarily diffused throughout the world from one single original stock.

12. See Hawkes 1969, pp. 21–4.

13. See Blom and Blom 1967.

14. The facts about the Chamula come mainly from my own research. But see also Pozas 1959.

15. See Mangelsdorf 1970.

16. See, for example, Woodburn 1968, p. 54.

17. From Lee and Devore 1968, frontispiece.

18. Harris, D. R. 1969.

19. See Willey 1971.

20. Richards 1939, p. 196.

21. Ibid, p. 46.

22. Ibid, p, 190.

23. Ibid, p. 252.

24. Ibid, p. 246.

25. Ibid, p. 77.

26. The best comprehensive definition of 'involution' is in Geertz 1970, p. 81, quoting from a study by A. Goldenweiser. My own definition of 'involution' is intended to be no more than a simplification, and adaptation, of Goldenweiser's.

27. Malinowski 1935, p. 59.

28. Ibid, p. 193.

29. Ibid, p. 392.

30. Ibid, p. 26.

31. Ibid, p. 29.

32. See Leach 1959.

33. This paragraph is based entirely on Geertz 1970.

34. For the ethnography of Kula see Malinowski 1932a, and for a political analysis, Uberoi 1962.

35. Mauss 1954.

36. Bohannan, L. 1958, p. 41, fig. 2.

37. Evans-Pritchard 1940, p. 203.

38. Geertz 1970, p. 36.

39. Lévi-Strauss 1969a, Chapter 29.

40. Malinowski 1935. See also Malinowski 1932b.

41. Personal observation in Kampala, Uganda.

42. Evans-Pritchard 1951, pp. 24–99. See also p. 23 above.

43. Firth 1936 and 1939.
44. Balikci 1968.
45. Durkheim 1933, Chapter Two.
46. Maquet 1964.
47. Stenning 1959.
48. The most creative analysis of caste is Dumont, L. 1972.
49. Durkheim 1933, Chapter Three.
50. Richards 1939. See also pp. 47–50 above.
51. Described in Bohannan and Bohannan 1968.
52. For the combination of trade with markets, see Polanyi, Arensberg and Pearson 1957.
53. I am, so far as I know, the only anthropologist to have studied Pantelhó.
54. Personal observation.
55. This is an example of the well-known Gresham's law, that 'the bad drives out the good'.
56. Godelier 1969.
57. This was a critical aspect of the run-away inflation of the Mark in Germany in the early 1920s.
58. See Douglas 1966, p. 69.
59. See Sayers 1949, p. 178.
60. The history of modern Britain and the United States contains many examples of such policies.
61. See Goody 1968 and p. 114 below.

CHAPTER 5

1. Page 8 above.
2. A large number of different studies on this theme are to be found in Mead 1937.
3. Durkheim 1915, p. 422.
4. Evans-Pritchard 1965, pp. 65–7 is an important case.
5. See Banton 1965 for a general study of roles.
6. Richards 1939, p. 196.
7. See Wilson 1951, Chapter VII.
8. Examples are given in Oberg 1940 and Richards 1940.
9. See Hart and Pelling 1960, pp. 1–4 'the first men in Australia'.
10. See page 76 above.
11. Bradbury 1957, p. 26.
12. See Wolf 1966.
13. A detailed study of such a migration is Butterworth 1970.
14. Bloch 1961, Chapter XVIII.
15. Frank 1967, p. 295.
16. Dumont, R. 1957, Chapter VII.
17. Leach 1962 shows how such an analysis of caste is inaccurate and highly prejudicial.
18. See page 69 above.
19. See Butterworth 1970.
20. Lewis 1960 is the most important.

21. This is a characteristic failure of bureaucracy: see page 38 above. The mountain communities of Appalachia are a special case of the 'culture of poverty' typifying a white Anglo-Saxon population.

22. See Origo 1963, p. 153.

23. This is the theme of Cancian 1965.

24. Deane 1968 is a seminal study on this question.

25. See Chapter 3, p. 36 above.

26. E.g. Van Velsen 1964, p. 12.

27. See Marx 1844.

28. For an evocative fictional study of this, see Sillitoe 1963.

CHAPTER 6

1. See Barton 1949.

2. See Fortes 1945, p. 106.

3. See Wilson 1951, p. 30.

4. Evans-Pritchard 1937. See also Chapter 8, below.

5. Vansina 1969.

6. See Hoebel 1954, Chapter 7.

7. Evans-Pritchard 1940, p. 162.

8. This, indeed, is a weakness of many advanced legal systems, including those of the United States and Great Britain.

9. Malinowski 1940, p. 126.

10. Fortes 1957.

11. Linton 1936, p. 115.

12. Described in Bohannan and Bohannan 1968. See also Chapter 4, p. 64 above.

13. Hart and Pelling 1960, p. 37.

14. See Van Velsen 1964.

15. See Lienhardt 1961.

16. Bohannan, P. 1957, Chapter II.

17. Leach 1954, p. 145.

18. Lowie 1956, pp. 22–3.

19. Bohannan, P. 1957, pp. 142–3.

20. Von Fürer-Haimendorff 1967, p. 76.

21. Evans-Pritchard 1940, pp. 152–64.

22. Hoebel 1954, Chapter 7.

23. Barton 1949.

24. Bohannan, P. 1957, Chapters IV to IX.

25. Gulliver 1963, Part Four.

26. Southall 1956.

27. Gluckman 1955, pp. 2, 3, 13.

28. Vansina 1969.

29. Hoebel 1954, pp. 164–7.

30. Dr. R. Abrahams, personal communication.

31. Fallers 1956 is a particular study of the Busoga of Uganda, based on this theme.

32. Associated particularly with Prof. Max Gluckman of the University of Manchester.

CHAPTER 7

1. The essence of his ideas is contained in de Saussure 1969.
2. Cowan 1964.
3. Carroll 1965, p. 191 gives an annotated version of this famous poem, suggesting actual English cognates for the nonsense words used, and including also French and German versions.
4. Leach 1964 gives an example for a primitive culture: Switzerland is one for a culture of an advanced society.
5. Richards 1939, p. 231.
6. Vendryès is a classic study on this theme.
7. See Chomsky 1965.
8. See especially the articles contained in Pride and Holmes 1972, Parts Two and Three.
9. For an essay which combines an anthropological with a literary approach to a particular French poem, see Jakobson and Lévi-Strauss 1962.
10. This slogan appears to have been superseded: this illustrates the preference in advertising for fleeting symbols. This whole subject is considered in depth, in relation to women's fashions, in Barthes 1967.
11. This theme is worked out, with numerous examples from contemporary life, in Barthes, 1967.
12. Described in Turner 1967, Chapter VII.
13. This whole process is the theme of Vansina 1966.
14. See Evans-Pritchard 1965, p. 5.
15. The leading modern study is Lévi-Strauss 1969: this starts out with a paradox, in that the author himself considers the category of 'totems' to be a false one.
16. Ibid, pp. 155–61.
17. See Chomsky 1965.
18. Lévi-Strauss 1969a, Chapter 2.
19. See Newnham and Lintung 1971.
20. See Goody 1968. It is astonishing that this recent book contains the first systematic treatment of literacy in an anthropological context. The introduction to it is the source of many of the ideas in the present chapter.
21. The transition has, however, been made by a number of writers, including the philosopher, Bertrand Russell, and the astronomer, Fred Hoyle.

CHAPTER 8

1. Durkheim 1915, pp. 38–42.
2. Turner 1967, Chapter IV.
3. Van Gennep 1960, Chapter IV.
4. Turner 1967, pp. 233, 254.
5. Lévi-Strauss 1969b, pp. 84–5.
6. See Malinowski 1954, Section III, 4, 'Death and the re-integration

of the group'. This whole theme is treated in great depth for one particular African tribe in Goody 1962.

7. An extreme case of simple technology is provided by the Guayaki Indians of Paraguay, who subsist almost entirely on wild honey, but who, none the less, use some thirty different tools and utensils: Musée de l'homme, Paris.

8. Significantly the special prayers in the Anglican Prayer Book (which was compiled more than 300 years ago) directed against such natural disasters, are hardly ever used at the present time.

9. Southall 1956, p. 95.

10. Lienhardt 1961, Chapter 5.

11. Krige and Krige 1954, p. 66.

12. Van Gennep 1960.

13. This is essentially because Christianity is an 'ethical' religion, in a sense which is explained on page 126 below. But the sacrament of extreme unction may be thought of as a (pre-)mortuary custom of the nature of a *rite de passage*. It is significant how often in history catholicism has seemed to look back to more primitive rites.

14. Fortes 1945, p. 31.

15. See 'Baloma; the spirits of the dead in the Trobriand islands' in Malinowski 1954, pp. 149-254.

16. Mercier 1954, p. 227.

17. For the symbolism of Ndembu circumcision, see Chapter 7, p. 109.

18. See Chapter 6, p. 91.

19. Forbidden by the third commandment; Exodus 20:4, and condemned by almost all the prophets of Israel.

20. Described in Horton 1962.

21. Described in Holas 1952.

22. This case is described in Evans-Pritchard 1937, an anthropological classic.

23. Described by Lienhardt 1961, pp. 10-27.

24. Ibid, p. 29.

25. Middleton 1960, pp. 79, 140.

26. The symbolism and ritual of the communion are examined in Chapter 7, p. 108.

27. This explains why so often the first action of missionaries in a new area is to reduce the local language to writing, translate the scriptures, and then teach as many people as possible to read them.

28. See 'The Righteousness of God', by E. G. Rupp and 'Martin Luther' by John M. Todd.

29. See Obeyesekere 1968.

30. Now 1900 years of Christian literacy have over-populated this world and so the present Pope, Paul VI, has had to banish from the calendar a number of popular Saints, Christopher, Nicholas, George and so on, to incorporate others, better recorded in history, such as Thomas More. This is almost an example of the anthropological concept of structural amnesia.

31. Such religious movements are the subject of Lanternari 1963. See also Burridge 1961, which more emphasizes millenarism in primitive societies.

32. Described in Worsley 1957.

CHAPTER 9

1. Best known for his monumental comparative study of certain aspects of primitive religion, 'The Golden Bough'.

2. See the books cited in the bibliography under Malinowski, to get some idea of the scope of his contribution to anthropology.

3. Lewis 1960.

4. Evans-Pritchard 1940.

5. Firth 1963, p. 1.

6. This issue is considered in numerous articles, mostly dealing with Latin America. See for example Mintz 1953 and Wolf 1957.

BIBLIOGRAPHY

BALICKI, A. 1968. *The Netsilik Eskimos. Adaptive Process*. In Lee and Devore pp. 78–82. New York, Natural History Press.

BANTON, M. ed. 1965. *Roles. An Introduction to the study of social relations*. New York, Basic Books.

BARNICOT, N. A. 1969. Human Nutrition: evolutionary perspectives. In Ucko and Dimbleby.

BARTHES, R. 1967. *Système de la Mode*. Paris. Editions du Seuil.

BARTHES, R. 1969. *Mythologies*. London, Jonathan Cape. New York, Hill and Wang.

BARTON, R. F. 1949. *The Kalingas: their institutions and custom law*. New York, AMS. Press.

BENDIX, R. 1966. *Max Weber. An intellectual portrait*. London, Methuen. Garden City New York, Doubleday.

BLOCH, M. 1961. *Feudal Society*. London, Routledge and Kegan Paul. University of Chicago Press.

BLOK, A. 1969. Peasant, patrons and brokers in Western Sicily. Anthropological Quarterly. Vol. 42. pp. 155–70.

BLOM, F. and BLOM, G. D. 1967. The Lacandones. In *Handbook of Middle-American Indians*, Vol. VII, Part I. Ethnography. University of Texas.

BOHANNAN, L. 1958. Political aspects of Tiv Social Organisation. In Middleton and Tait.

BOHANNAN, P. 1957. *Judgement and Justice among the Tiv*. London, Oxford University Press.

BOHANNAN, P. and BOHANNAN, L. 1968. *Tiv Economy*. Chicago, Northwestern University African Studies.

BOHANNAN, P. and MIDDLETON, J. 1968. *Marriage Family and Residence*. New York, Natural History Press.

BOISSEVAIN, J. F. 1968. The place of non-groups in the social sciences. Man N.S. Vol. 3. pp. 524–56.

BRADBURY, R. E. 1957. *The Benin Kingdom*. London, International African Institute.

BURNS, T. ed. 1969 *Industrial Man*. London and Baltimore, Penguin.

BURRIDGE, K. 1969. *New Heaven, New Earth*. London, Pavilion Books. New York, Schocken Books.

BUTTERWORTH, D. 1970. From royalty to poverty: the decline of a rural Mexican community. Human Organisation. Vol. 29. p. 5.

CANCIAN, F. 1969. *Economics and Prestige in a Maya Community*. Stanford California, University Press.

CARROLL, L. 1965. Alice through the looking-glass. In *The Annotated Alice*. London, Penguin. New York, Potter.

CHOMSKY, N. 1965. *Aspects of the Theory of Syntax*. Cambridge, Massachusetts Institute of Technology.

COHEN, Y. 1968. *Man in Adaptation: The Cultural Present*. Chicago. Aldine Atherton.

COWAN, G. M. 1964. Mazateco whistled speach in Hymes, D. q.v.

DEANE, P. M. 1966. *The First Industrial Revolution*. Cambridge and New York, Cambridge University Press.

DEVORE, I. and Washburn S. L. 1968. Baboon Ecology and Human Evolution. In Cohen, Y. q.v.

DOUGLAS, M. M. 1966. *Purity and Danger*. London, Routledge and Kegan Paul. New York, Praeger.

DOUGLAS, M. M. 1969. Is matrimony doomed in Africa? In Douglas and Kaberry, q.v.

DOUGLAS, M. M. and KABERRY, M. 1969. *Man in Africa*. London, Tavistock. New York, Barnes and Noble.

DUMONT, L. 1972. *Homo Hierarchicus*. London, Paladin. University of Chicago Press.

DUMONT, R. 1957. *Types of Rural Economy*. London, Methuen. New York, Barnes and Noble.

DURKHEIM, E. 1915. *The Elementary Forms of the Religious Life*. London, Allen and Unwin. New York, Humanities Press.

DURKHEIM, E. 1933. *The Division of Labour in Society*. London, Macmillan. Riverside, New Jersey, The Free Press.

EVANS-PRITCHARD, E. E. 1937. *Witchcraft, Oracles and Magic among the Azande*. London and New York, Oxford University Press.

EVANS-PRITCHARD, E. E. 1940. *The Nuer*. London and New York, Oxford University Press.

EVANS-PRITCHARD, E. E. 1951. *Kinship and Marriage among the Nuer*. London and New York, Oxford University Press.

EVANS-PRITCHARD, E. E. 1962. *Essays in Social Anthropology*. London, Faber and Faber. Riverside, New Jersey, The Free Press.

EVANS-PRITCHARD, E. E. 1965. *Theories of Primitive Religion*. London and New York, Oxford University Press.

FALLERS, L. A. 1965. *A Bantu Bureaucracy*. Cambridge University Press. Chicago University Press.

FIRTH, J. R. 1936 *We, the Tikopia*. London, Allen and Unwin. Boston, Beacon Press.

FIRTH, J. R. 1939. *Primitive Polynesian Economy*. London, Routledge and Sons.

FIRTH, J. R. 1963. *Elements of Social Organisation*. Glasgow, Watts and Co. Gloucester, Mass. Peter Smith.

FORDE, D. 1954. ed. *African Worlds*. Oxford University Press.

FORTES, M. 1940. The political systems of the Tallensi of the northern territories of the Gold Coast. In Fortes and Evans-Pritchard. q.v.

FORTES, M. 1945. *The Dynamics of Clanship among the Tallensi*. Oxford University Press. New York, Humanities Press.

FORTES, M. 1957. *The Web of Kinship among the Tallensi*. London, Cambridge University Press.

FORTES, M. and EVANS-PRITCHARD, E. E. 1940. Ed. *African Political Systems*. London and New York, Oxford University Press.

Fox, R. 1967. *Kinship and Marriage*. London and Baltimore, Pelican.

Frank, A. G. 1967. *Capitalism and Underdevelopment in Latin America*. New York, Monthly Review Press.

Frazer, J. G. 1922. *The Golden Bough*. London and Riverside, New Jersey, Macmillan.

Von Furer-Haimendorff, C. 1967. *Morals and Merit*. London, Weidenfeld and Nicholson. University of Chicago Press.

Geertz, C. 1970. *Agricultural Involution*. Berkeley and Los Angeles, University of California Press.

Gluckman, M. 1955. *The Judicial Process among the Barotse of Northern Rhodesia*. Glencoe, Illinois, The Free Press.

Gluckman, M. 1955. *Custom and Conflict in Africa*. London and New York, Oxford University Press.

Godelier, M. 1969. *La Monnaie de Sel des Bariya de Nouvelle Guinee*. Paris, L'Homme. IX, 2, p. 5.

Goody, J. R. 1958, ed., *The Development Cycle in Domestic Groups*. London, Cambridge University Press.

Goody, J. R. 1962. *Death, Property and the Ancestors*. London, Tavistock. Stanford California, Stanford University Press.

Goody, J. R. 1968. *Literacy in Traditional Societies*. London and New York, Cambridge University Press.

Gough, G. K. 1968. The Nayars and the definition of marriage. In Bohannan and Middleton. q.v.

Gulliver, P. H. 1963. *Social Control in an African Society*. London, Routledge and Kegan Paul. New York, New York University Press.

Harris, D. R. 1969. Agricultural systems, ecosystems and the origins of agriculture. In Ucko and Dimbleby. q.v.

Harris, M. 1959. The economy has no surplus. American Anthropologist. Vol. 61, p. 185.

Hart, C. W. M. and Pelling, A. R. 1959. *The Tiwi of North Australia*. New York, Holt, Rinehart and Winston.

Hawkes, J. G. 1969. The ecological background of plant domestication. In Ucko and Dimbleby.

Hoebel, E. A. 1954. *The Law of Primitive Man*. Cambridge, Mass.' Harvard University Press.

Holas, B 1952. *Les Masques Kono: leur rôle dans la vie politique et religieuse*. Paris.

Horton, R. 1962. The Kalabari World-view. An outline and interpretation. Africa 1962. Vol. XXXII, pp. 197–219.

Hymes, D. 1964, ed. *Language in Culture and Society*. New York, Harper and Row.

Jakobson, R. and Levi-Strauss, C. 1962. 'Les Chats' de Charles Baudelaire. Paris, L'Homme. II, I, pp. 5–21.

Krige, J. D. and Krige, E. J. 1954. The Lovedu of the Transvaal. In Forde, q.v.

Lanternari, G. 1963. *The Religions of the Oppressed*. London, Macgibbon and Kee. New York, New American Library.

Leach, E. R. 1954. *Political Systems of Highland Burma*. London School of Economics, Monograph on Social Anthropology. New York, Humanities Press.

LEACH, E. R. 1959. Hydraulic Society in Ceylon. Past and Present. Vol. 15, pp. 2–25.

LEACH, E. R. 1961. *Rethinking Anthropology*. London School of Economics, Monograph on Social Anthropology. New York, Humanities Press.

LEACH, E. R. 1962, ed. *Aspects of Caste*. London, Cambridge University Press.

LEACH, E. R. 1968, ed. *Dialectic In Practical Religion*. London, Cambridge University Press.

LEE, R. B. 1968. What hunters do for a living or how to make out on scarce resources. In Lee and Devore, q.v.

LEE, R. B. and DEVORE, I. 1968, eds. *Man the hunter*. Chicago, Aldine.

LÉVI-STRAUSS, C. 1956. *Tristes Topiques*. Paris, 1964. New York, Atheneum.

LÉVI-STRAUSS, C. 1967. *L'Origine de Manieres de Table*. Paris, Plon.

LÉVI-STRAUSS, C. 1969a *The Elementary Structure of Kinship*. London, Eyre and Spottiswood. Boston, Mass., Beacon Press.

LÉVI-STRAUSS, C. 1969b *The Raw and the Cooked*. London, Jonathan Cape. New York, Harper and Row.

LÉVI-STRAUSS, C. 1969c *Totemism*. London, Pelican. Boston, Beacon Press.

LEWIS, O. 1960. *The Children of Sanchez*. London, Penguin. New York, Random House.

LIENHARDT, R. G. 1961. *Divinity and Experience*. London and New York, Oxford University Press.

LINTON, R. 1936. *The Study of Man*. New York, Appleton-Century-Croft Inc.

LOWIE, R. H. 1956 *The Crow Indians*. New York, Holt, Rinehart and Winston.

MAINE, H. 1961. *Ancient Law*. London, John Murray, and 1931, New York, Dutton.

MAIR, L. 1962. *Primitive Government*. London and Baltimore, Pelican.

MALINOWSKI, B. 1932a, *Argonauts of the Western Pacific*. London, Allen and Unwin. New York, Dutton.

MALINOWSKI, B. 1932b, *The Sexual Life of Savages in North Western Melanesia*. London, Routledge and Kegan Paul. New York, Harcourt Brace Jovanovich.

MALINOWSKI, B. 1935. *Coral Gardens and their Magic*. London, Allen and Unwin.

MALINOWSKI, B. 1940. *Crime and Custom in Savage Society*. London, Kegan Paul Trench and Truler and Co. New York, Humanities Press.

MALINOWSKI, B. 1954. *Magic, Science and Religion and other essays*. New York, Doubleday.

MANGELSDORF, P. C. 1970. The mystery of corn. Scientific American, pp. 2–6.

MAQUET, J. J. 1954. The Kingdom of Ruanda. In Forde, q.v.

MARX, K. 1844. Alienated Labour. In Burns, q.v.

MAUSS, M. 1954. *The Gift*. London, Cohen and West. New York, W. W. Norton.

MEAD, M. 1935. *Sex and Temperament in Three Primitive Societies*.

London, George Routledge and Sons. Gloucester, Mass. Peter Smith.

MEAD, M. 1937, ed. *Cooperation and Competition among Primitive Peoples.* New York, McGraw-Hill.

MERCIER, P. 1954. The Fon of Dahomey. In Forde, q.v.

MIDDLETON, J. 1960. *Lugbara Religion.* London and New York, Oxford University Press.

MIDDLETON, J. and TAIT, D. 1958. *Tribes without Rulers.* London, Routledge and Kegan Paul. New York, Humanities Press.

MINTZ, S. W. 1953. The folk-urban continuum and the rural proletarian economy. American Journal of Sociology. Vol. 59, pp. 136–45.

NEWCOMER, P. J. 1972. The Nuer are Dinka: an essay on origins and environmental determinism. Man. New Series, Vol. 17, p. 5.

NEWNHAM, R. and LINTUNG, T. 1971. *About Chinese.* London and Baltimore, Pelican.

Notes and Queries in Anthropology. 1951. 6th Edition. London and Boston, Routledge and Kegan Paul.

OBERG, K. 1940. The kingdom of Ankole in Uganda. In Fortes and Evans-Pritchard, q.v.

ORIGO, IRIS. 1963. *The Merchant of Prato.* London, Peregrine.

POLANYI, K., ARENSBERG, C. M. and PEARSON, H. W. 1957, eds. *Trade and Market in the Early Empires.* Chicago, The Free Press.

POZAS, R. 1959 Chamula—un pueblo indiano de los altos de Chiapas. Mexico Instituto Nacional indigeuista.

PRIDE, J. B. and HOLMES, J. 1972, eds. *Socio-linguistics.* London, Penguin.

RADCLIFFE-BROWN, A. R. and FORDE, D. 1950, eds. *African Systems of Kinship and Marriage.* London, Oxford University Press.

RICHARDS, A. I. 1939. *Land Labour and Diet in Northern Rhodesia.* London and New York, Oxford University Press.

RICHARDS, A. I. 1940. The political system of the Bemba tribe in North Eastern Rhodesia. In Fortes and Evans-Pritchard, q.v.

RIVERS, W. H. C. 1906. *The Todas.* London, Macmillan. New York, Humanities Press.

RUZ, A. and VOGT, E. Z. 1971, eds. *Desarollo Cultural de los Mayas.* Mexico, D.F. Universidad Nacional de Mexico.

SAUSSURE, F. de. 1966. *Course in General Linguistics.* New York, McGraw-Hill.

SAYERS, D. L. 1949, trs. and ed. *Dante: The Divine Comedy.* London and Baltimore, Penguin.

SILLITOE, A. 1959. *Saturday Night, Sunday Morning.* London, Pan Books. New York, Alfred Knopf.

SMITH, R. T. 1956. *The Negro Family in British Guiana.* London, Routledge and Kegan Paul. New York, Humanities Press.

STENNING, D. J. 1959. *Savannah Nomads.* London, Oxford University Press.

TURNBULL, C. M. Z. 1965. *Wayward Servants: The Two Worlds of the African Pigmies.* Garden City, New York, Natural History Press.

TURNER, V. 1967. *The Forest of Symbols.* Ithaca, New York, Cornell University Press.

UBEROI, J. P. S. 1962. *The Politics of the Kula Ring.* Manchester University Press. New York, Humanities Press.

Ucko, P. J. and Dimbleby, G. W. 1969. *The Domestication and Exploitation of Plants and Animals*. London, Duckworth. Chicago, Aldine Atherton.

Van Gennep, A. 1960. *The Rites of Passage*. London, Routledge and Kegan Paul.

Vansina, J. 1966. *Oral Tradition*. London, Chicago, Aldine Atherton.

Vansina, J. 1969. The Bushong Poison Ordeal. In Douglas and Kaberry, q.v.

Van Velsen, J. 1964. *The Politics of Kinship*. Manchester University Press. New York, Humanities Press.

Willey, G. R. 1971. An archaeological frame of reference for Maya culture history. In Ruz and Vogt, q.v.

Wilson, M. 1951. *Good Company*. Oxford University Press. Gloucester, Mass., Peter Smith.

Wolf, E. R. 1957. Closed corporate peasant communities in Meso-America and Central Java. South Western Journal of Anthropology, Vol. 68, pp. 1236–44.

Wolf, E. R. 1966. *Peasants*. Englewood Cliffs, New Jersey, Prentice-Hall.

Woodburn, J. 1968. An introduction to Hadza ecology. In Lee and Devore, q.v.

Worsley, P. 1957. *The Trumpet Shall Sound*. London, Macgibbon and Kee. New York, Schocken Books.

Yablonsky, L. 1967. *The Violent Gang*. London, Pelican Books. New York, Collier–Macmillan.

INDEX